MAN NUP

A Groom's Complete Guide to Heroic Wedding Planning

by

RICK WEBB

All rights reserved

Published in the United States

Copyright © 2016 by Rick Webb

http://www.rickwebb.net/man-nup/

Library of Congress Cataloging-in-Publication-Data
is available upon request.

Printed in the United States of America

Cover design by Emma Webb

For Emma

First photograph taken by Storytellers & Co. Second photo by Eric Harvey Brown of Honey and Moon Photography. Used with generous permission.

Table of Contents

Chapter 1: A Man's Job

Why This Book?

When I began planning my wedding, in late 2012, I had never heard of another man planning his own wedding. Since then, I've seen two other male friends plan their own weddings, and have met several other people who've done so as well. Is it a real trend? Three's a trend, right? Stats are hard to come by. But is it so crazy to imagine? Gender roles are changing, or being reassigned. The manner in which any two people in a couple relate to one another and make things work is varied and infinite. The times are a changin', and can't part of that change include some men taking tasks that have been traditionally assigned to women? My friend Mike, who also planned his own wedding, "I think it's sad that the wedding industry is so focused on women, as if men don't care about the biggest day of their lives too." Well no longer!

Speaking of Mike, throughout this book, in addition to my telling you what I've learned, you're going to hear from three other men who have planned their own weddings – Mike, Richard and Ryan. Wedding planning is a highly social task, in which dozens of people participate. But at its core, much like the Highlander, there can be only one. Someone has to be in charge of the day-to-day planning. You're either in a support role, or *are* the planner. Being in a support role to your spouse as she plans the wedding is a very different act than planning it yourself. This is also true if you choose to hire a wedding planner to handle the grunt work for you from beginning to end. You and your spouse then move into the support roles.

If you are in a support role, this book will still prove useful. You'll pick up the basics, and learn how to avoid common wedding planning pitfalls and traps (and boy, there are a lot of 'em). You'll learn about the digital tools that are out there to make your wedding planning simpler. In fact, I'd venture say you'll be much more useful to your future spouse having read this book, even if you're not the primary planner.

But if you *are* the planner, this book is for you.

Other Wedding Planning Books

Now why, in this day and age, does a man planning a wedding necessitate a different kind of wedding planning book? Is this a book full of gender stereotyping and dick jokes? No, and no. What I found while planning a wedding as a man is that many of the wedding planning how-to books out there provided only minimal value. They focused unduly on factors of wedding planning that I didn't care about, while completely ignoring areas that were of importance (or a complete mystery) to me. They assumed I knew things I didn't know, and didn't know things I did.

Some of this may be gender-based, but I also believe that some of it's an aspect of the wedding in-dustrial complex. The wedding industry is designed from the ground up to make you feel insecure about your decisions, and to invoke fear in order to get you to throw more money at a particular aspect of the production. I'll be blunt – there is no freaking dif-ference between the many different types of frosting for your cake. It doesn't matter. Half the crap people want you to buy for weddings has no value or utility whatsoever. The brainwashing of the wedding indus-trial complex starts out with the wedding planning books, and this is a book designed to avoid all of that.

This book does not (completely) replace a traditional wedding planning book. What this book is is an appendix – a corollary – to traditional wed-ding planning books. There are no detailed sections on fondant icing vs. butter cream. I couldn't tell you that if my life depended on it. Most wedding planning books will make you feel like your life depended on it. Part of me is tempted to say you shouldn't bother with traditional wedding planning books at all. They can make you crazy. They can convince you that chargers are important, and choosing one is a monumental task. I strongly suspect that at this moment, you don't know what a charger is or how it relates to weddings. This is good. This is as it should be.

Let's get this out of the way: a charger is a plate that you put underneath your plate. It sits there, unused, until they take it away. No, I am not kidding.

When I planned my wedding, I bought a wedding planning book online. I just Googled "wedding planning books" and bought one of the top links. I read through it, and honestly, I didn't feel like it helped me too much. It went on and on about topics which were not of interest to me, like flower types and flatware, and spoke very little about things that I was stressed about, like what exactly I would need to rent from the rental company, and whether I was committing some giant breach of protocol by using Paperless Post.

All that being said, my advice is to splurge the $10 on some normal wedding planning book. I know, I know, I contradict myself. I contain Whitman-esque multitudes. But buying a cheap wedding book is probably, on balance, worth it. It'll help you learn the lingo, so to speak, and get a sense of what other people think is important. The non-traditional nature of this book is, one presumes, why you purchased it. But as unconventional as you may be, there are other people involved in this whole process, and even if you're going to roundly and categorically reject tradition, you should probably know, exactly, what traditions you are rejecting. Did you know, for example, that flower girls are traditionally girls and ring bearers are traditionally boys? I did not know that. I was a flower girl myself when I was six so WHO KNEW. When we decided to have an adult man be our flower bearer, it was good to know we were choosing to be weird. Best to know these things. This lead me to realize that traditional wedding books DO, in fact, have a use: they should be thought of as translation dictionaries. Sort of a "normal-person-to-wedding-obsessor-dictionary."

What to Expect

So what should you expect as a man planning his own wedding?

There's the obvious. Much of what a woman experiences when planning her wedding, you will experience too. It's a ton of extra work on top of the rest of your life. You'll feel the burn in your pocketbook, and you'll feel the burn in your free time.

Let's play a bit to gender stereotypes here. Men are not always known as being the most organized. They can procrastinate. Both of these traits are death when it comes to wedding planning. Procrastination and disorganization mean extra costs. You'll also probably need to stay on top of them way earlier than you may think you need to. Part of this is practical. If you're rich, great. If not, your innate tendency to put things off will cost you money.

But it's more than that. Your spouse-to-be will probably want to know you're on top of things. Even if they don't want a thing to do with the wedding, future spouses will seek comfort in knowing that you're taking care of it all. This means you'll generally want to have things taken care of before your better half thinks to ask about them. This means you'll want to have things taken care of long before you, personally, will think you'll need to.

Even if your betrothed is completely chillaxed and not worried about things at all, SOMEONE in the family is going to be curious and eager. They're going to ask questions. "When's the wedding?" "Where's the wedding?" "Is Joey coming?" It'll make your life, much, much easier to have answers to these questions. Not only will having an answer, again, convey the impression that you're on top of things, it will also shut down any potential avenue for family and friends offering unwanted input.

For know this: you're going to get a metric ton

of unwanted input. Everyone is gonna have an opinion. Friends, family, your better half's family, coworkers, strangers on the street. People you are meeting for the first time. Your single friends will be sick of hearing you talk about the wedding, and your married friends and acquaintances will seem to want to talk about nothing else.

The fact of the matter is, however, that a lot of people are *obsessed* with weddings. You're going to have to talk about your wedding a lot. I tried various approaches to this. When some friend or family member would come up and gush and ask me cooing questions about aisle runners or something, at first I would try and be a little dismissive and say something like "oh man, all that stuff is pointless, who cares." But you know, I just felt like I was shooting them down. They wanted to live vicariously, and hear all about it.

So, when a well-wisher asked me about aisle runners, rather than saying "oh man, who cares," I would learn that instead I should say "well the venue is just so lovely, and they have these nice end ornaments on their pews blah blah blah so we thought we'd take that money and spend it on a better meal." Or literally any other aspect of the wedding. Because they don't really care about any particular facet of the wedding, they just want to talk about it. You could say "yeah we just walked into the bakery and bought the cheapest cake," and deflate their spirits, or you acould say "oh, it's spice cake with raspberry filling and fondant icing," and both would be totally true. May as well learn the lingo and keep people happy.

For the next year of your life, people are gonna say congratulations. They're going to ask "when's the wedding." They're being polite. They don't really care. I find it's best to develop some boring stock answers and stick to them. Beware of jokes: people may spread rumors around them, believe them, expect them. If you think that this particular coworker or cocktail conversational partner might have some knowledge about nuptial logistics, feel free to ask them for their advice. Try to have a little fun with their endless, eternal questioning, and maybe get something out of it. Don't fret too much about their reactions or opinions (since everyone is going to have one). It'll be a part of your life for quite some time. HUNDREDS of people are going to ask you this.

Ryan, who planned his own wedding, reminds us that there's a point to all of this. "TRY. Even the slightest bit of effort or sincerity will win you favor with your spouse, your family, and your friends, even if you're faking it. Everyone knows you don't care about table runners or what shape of tie your groomsmen will wear (or maybe you do, and you're a rockstar), but you earn points for trying. And maybe your fiancé will appreciate you for it / finally stop bothering you about the goddamned dinner plates. And maybe one of your guests will comment on how much she liked the banana leaves in the floral arrangements and how they so elegantly hid the stems but didn't block the candlelight. Whatever. At least someone will appreciate the effort, and you will actually get credit for something at your wedding, which is a small victory, but a victory nonetheless. Try."

(This line of questioning will transition, from the day you're married onward, for at least the next year, to the inquiry "how's married life?" Again, people don't really care. Just say that you're having less sex. Cut off the inevitable follow up inquiry about having babies by saying "never." The more quickly you cut off every. single. person's belief they have rights to some sort of inquiry about your baby-making plans, the better.)

In terms of being the planner of this wedding, you can expect much confusion from potential vendors. More than one vendor assumed I was a gay bear wedding planner, and my friend Ali, who was helping me out, was the bride. This made for many comically misdirected questions and much confusion. Once vendors and salespeople cotton to the fact that you're the groom, and you're doing the planning, they will be slightly confused. Most vendors have a whole sales approach, and it invariably revolves around preying on the bride's insecurities, hopes, dreams and childhood fantasies. This is not to say that men do not have insecurities, childhood fantasies or hopes and dreams, but rather that most vendors don't know how to wheedle their way into them. One of two things will happen at this point. They will simply shut down with the cognitive dissonance of you not being a woman, and they will proceed to act the same way they always do, trying to sell things to you as if you're the bride, or they will look for any means possible to establish communication with the "actual bride."

They want to talk to the bride because they assume they will be able to sell her upgrades more easily. Considering you and your bride decided that you were the one planning this wedding there may well be no need for this vendor to talk to the bride. This, I have found, is perhaps the single biggest benefit of having the groom plan the wedding. No one knows how to trap the groom and stick him with unwanted add-ons and extra expenses. Again, this is not to say that men are not susceptible to sales pressure, but rather the industry is not set up to exploit the psychological weaknesses more prominent in men. This varies by vendor type. Florists are less capable salespeople to men than caterers, for example.

Finally, know this: before, after and during the wedding, everyone will assume that the "bride" did all the planning (if you're straight). This is okay. Let them think it. Anything we can do to shine more light onto our loved ones, right?

A Note On Gender Pronouns

Gender pronouns for this book are a tricky business. Typically, when writing about an unknown third person, I, like many writers today, like to use the pronoun "she," in absence of a gender neutral pronoun in the English language. We do this because we like to feel inclusive.

However, in the course of writing a men's wedding planning book, the gender pronoun "she" actually takes on some potentially non-inclusive connotations. That is, we are big supporters of gay marriage, and believe this book is useful for men planning their weddings, whether they are gay or straight.

Additionally, the terms "bride" and "groom," then take on some challenges as well. When two men marry, is there a bride? Is there a groom? For that matter, which are you?

Since we're blazing a bit of a new trail here, we've chosen, for clarity's sake, to assume that you are the groom, and you are marrying a bride. We've made efforts to avoid gendered pronouns for your future mate. Note, however, that there are sections where this is more difficult, such as when talking about wedding dresses. Though hey, maybe you're a dude wearing a wedding dress. Your day is going to be awesome, too. So, please note that while we've attempted to use "she" and "her" sparingly, there have been a few spots where it may be unavoidable.

We've also included two interviews with two male wedding planners, and asked them about any differences or gotchas between straight weddings and gay weddings. You'll see that the answers generally lie in the realm of "it's all about the two individuals." In short, appropriate whatever customs you feel comfortable with. Says Jeremy, one of the planners: "I myself am throwing a bouquet at my wedding and no one's stopping me." Amen.

Onward!

Chapter 2: Getting Started

Why Are You Doing This

If you're planning your wedding, it's important to understand why. That is, not why you're getting married – hopefully you have that worked out, and if not, this isn't the book for you – but why you're doing the planning. Perhaps you're trying to make your wife's life easier. She may be nervous about the ceremony and, because you love her, you want to take a bunch of responsibilities off her plate. Perhaps you're the more organized person in the relationship. Perhaps you or your family is paying for the wedding and it makes more logistical sense for you to handle the details.

Whatever the reason, internalize it, absorb it, don't forget it. Different reasons will have different levels of autonomy and different levels of coordination with your future spouse and other people. For my part, my wife Emma didn't want to deal with wedding planning at all. When we were talking about what getting married meant to us, I told her that if we were going to get married, the act of witnessing to my friends and our community was very important to me. That I wanted to get up in front of everyone and say "I am serious about this relationship and this woman." This meant that I wanted to have a relatively large wedding – the friends and community being present was important so that I could state my vows in front of them. Emma didn't mind having a large wedding so long as she didn't have to deal with the logistics of it, which caused her anxiety.

This then, became my M.O. It was my guiding principle that I was doing this to save Emma the stress and extra work of planning a large wedding. Thus things that would have needed to be done for a wedding of any size – her dress, an officiant, whatnot – were things I consulted with her more on. Conversely, regarding topics that were specific to a large wedding – equipment rentals, live music, special insurance riders – I consulted with her less.

You will need to find your own balance, and this will be derived from your motivations for being the wedding planner. Remember this, for one of the biggest challenges in planning a wedding is striking the right balance of input from the non-planning member of the couple. Too little, and they will feel neglected, or not get the wedding they dreamed of. Too much, and they will feel overwhelmed and stressed, and your work to alleviate their stress will have been for nought.

Man Nup

What Matters

There exists a whole host of traditions and subconscious assumptions in our society about what the groom has to do when the bride plans the wedding. We've seen countless movies and TV shows where the groom is barraged with a seemingly endless series of questions on minutiae as his eyes glaze over. The cliché of grooms whispering conspiratorially to one another about how they just say "yes dear" to all questions is firmly entrenched in American society. Because of these widespread social mores and habits, it's not impossible for a bride and groom to get through a wedding planned by the bride without ever really discussing the groom's role. Say yes. Point at things. Dress well. Show up. Write a check. Don't get too drunk at the bachelor party. Or the wedding.

The same cannot be said of the reverse, however. You are part of a brave, rare posse of individuals who are blazing a trail, blah blah. Whatever. There's not necessarily any nobility in you planning this wedding (though believe me, several people are going to compliment you on your bravery and consideration). Nor are there any real conventions. The field is wide open. Roles and traditions have yet to be invented, so you get to help make them up. Lucky you.

What there is, however, is a profound need for you and your future spouse to work out, in advance, what you will be responsible for, and what aspects of the ritual in which they expect to participate.

I did this by having Emma write down a list. I had her write down everything that was important to her about the wedding in which she wanted input. She cared about her dress, obviously. She also wanted to be consulted on the music, and the cake/cupcakes. She exhibited a mild curiosity towards the food, and expressed a strong desire for a certain type of decoration (white stars). She had a few opinions about flowers. She wanted to give a final OK on the venue, so she she gave her opinions on the broad parameters about the venue. She wasn't concerned about choosing one specific venue over another that fit the bill. Other than these specific things, which were added to the list, she really didn't care about the details. She was utterly indifferent to the booze, the equipment rental, which specific caterer, other decorations, the exact schedule – that sort of thing.

This is a very worthwhile exercise that you and your betrothed should approach with honesty. Be thorough. Go through the topics in this book, and ask your mate whether or not they care about each item, and how much. Since you're a man planning a wedding, there is a good chance that you got to this point because your partner doesn't especially want the hassle or even care about many of these things.

However, it's been my experience that everyone has some level of care and desired participation. It's one thing to not want to see an endless litany of chargers, pew rails and bouquets. It's another to not have an opinion on where your wedding is actually located. Find out what's important to your betrothed and make a list. Agree upon these things in advance.

Now, it is natural in the course of the process for someone to change their mind on a few of these. There were places where, as the event grew near, Emma would come to realize she did, actually, have an opinion about something. That is totally okay if both parties understand the ground rules: it may be too late, it may be unchangeable, etc. It's important to not make it personal, and not get too upset that your partner (or you, for that matter) couldn't perfectly predict their opinions and emotions on a very large event both logistically and emotionally, a year in advance.

Another thing I found useful is to learn to distinguish between helpful suggestions and things that really matter to your partner. Emma would often say "oh we should do this or that!" I would misinterpret the suggestion as a new requirement, and go to town trying to make it happen. This was often a good thing, but in some cases it wasn't at all necessary, since Emma was just expressing excitement, or trying to be helpful. It's important to be able to discuss each of these things: is this a suggestion? Is it a new requirement? Is it something that is suddenly important to you? or are you just trying to be helpful?

Have an Angle

When starting wedding planning, you are going to need some guiding principles. You're going to need an angle. What is important to you about this wedding? What do you care about the most? Do you want a theme? Is a destination important? Write down a list of 3-4 things that are most important to you.

In addition to being useful in negotiation and planning with your spouse, this exercise is important for several reasons. It's important that you don't waste a lot of time investigating venues and vendors that may not fit in with what's important about your wedding. It also allows you to focus on what matters. It allows you to know where to apply the most resources in your budget, and where you are more comfortable making compromises. It allows you to give guidance to a professional planner, should you hire one (we will turn to this matter in a bit in Wedding Planners). Finally, it gives a guiding principle to all of your vendors – especially if what's important to you is some sort of theme. You may not be on hand to make every single individual decision. By having a "charter," if you will, those who do make decisions in your absence will know what's important.

"Rock wedding in space." "Romantic French getaway." "Small and intimate." Whatever it is, let this be your charter. Your vision. This is the talisman from which all major decisions flow. Not only will this make decision-making vastly easier, it will also make your wedding more coherent, charming, and stylish.

A word of "encouragement" from friend and fellow planning-man Mike:

> "Your family will hate everything you decide to do. The more you're pissing your family off the more you know your wedding will be yours."

If you're someone who likes to plan in advance, what I found to be incredibly useful was taking quick notes at all the weddings I went to in the year prior to my wedding. Location wasn't that important to me, nor was theme. I would go to weddings and I would jot down what I liked about them and what I didn't like about them. What I wanted to do differently. What was great. I ended up with a list of three key points that mattered to me: I wanted the whole event to be in one venue – no separate venue for ceremony vs. reception. I wanted the party to go late – as late as anyone would let us go. Finally, I wanted to avoid assigned seats in a sit down dinner. These were just my personal preferences – not necessarily those of my future spouse. In the end, she was cool with all of these, but even if she hadn't, this would have been a useful exercise, in order to quickly work out our concerns and reach a compromise before any major planning was done.

One of the first things you should do after deciding on what's important to the two of you is to start a Pinterest board of visual inspiration that reinforces, or exemplifies, your vision for your wedding. We'll talk about Pinterest in a bit, but what's important here is you begin collecting these visual examples. They do not need to be confined to photographs of weddings or examples of wedding prints. Matchbooks, advertisements, menus from restaurants, store signage – anything that you think falls in line with your vision of your wedding.

As we've said, Emma did the same, letting me know what was important to her. Luckily, our lists were compatible. If they weren't, we would have needed to do some negotiating. Better to do it earlier and work it out.

The Budget

You're going to need a budget. You're going to need to figure how much you can afford for this wedding. Determine a number. Write it down.

Now. This number. Speak not of it to anyone. Ever. When asked, give them a number that is 30% lower than this actual, real number. Every single person in the wedding industry, when you tell them your budget, is mentally adding 25% in their head. They know you are going to go over. And you are going to go over. It's best to accept it right away, have the number you tell people and the real number, and don't ever, ever admit it. Mike is even more blunt: "Quadruple any number that's in your head the moment after you ask her to marry you. Then quadruple that."

From this number, you're going to need to do rough ball-parking for everything in the wedding. The reception's venue food and drink will require about half of your budget – perhaps more if you're using separate venues for the ceremony and reception. Allocate somewhere around 5% for the dress. Other items: 10% for the rehearsal dinner, 5% for equipment rentals, 10% for decor and flowers (yes, seriously). Entertainment, 5-10%. Photography, 10%. You'll notice that adds up to 100%, and doesn't include the rings, gifts, transportation, hair and makeup. Adjust accordingly and block out the budget thusly. Give priority to the items that were related to your "most important things" list, and lower the allocation for those that are of less important. Don't forget tips.

If you're planning this whole wedding, then

there will be plenty of wiggle room as you procure various goods and services. The one thing you'll need to block out separately, however, is the bride's dress, shoes, and other garb. Let her manage that budget. More on that later. But if you're planning the rest, you can move money around as you go forward. Like we said, this is ballpark.

Discuss this number with your future spouse. Decide together. Especially if you two are paying for the wedding together.

Who's Paying

This may sound paradoxical, but one of the greatest pleasures of planning our wedding was the fact that I was also paying for it. The power of this cannot be overstated. No one – save my future wife – felt empowered to offer opinions and suggestions on how our wedding should be. I was a male wedding planner, I was paying for the wedding, and I am known to be somewhat stubborn. There was virtually no avenue of attack for busybody friends and relatives to insinuate themselves into the equation. No option for bribery, guilt tripping, or pouting. There were certain individuals who would try, and with certain others you could literally see the calculations going on behind their eyes trying to find a way in, but there was no path available to them. It saved a lot of stress and drama. And I have a relatively drama-free family. But when someone else is paying, someone else has some control. They can try and tell you where to have the wedding. When. What city. They can insist on inviting 10-20 people you don't even know. Ask yourself if it's worth it. Think twice about it.

It should go without saying that many of us do not have the financial freedom to take on the whole wedding themselves, and your family might be the world's least dramatic, must blindly supportive family in the world. According to a poll from theknot.com, a mere 37% of American couples plan on financially contributing to their wedding[1]. The actual number is probably higher (budget wedding planners probably aren't hanging out on theknot.com as much), but there is no shame in receiving assistance.

If you think it's safe to have someone help you financially with the wedding, by all means, go for it. It's important to understand, however, that with money often comes conditions, or at least opinions. When taking money from family, endeavor to make it explicit that money does not buy control. They may still try, but having them agree outright that the decisions are in your hands is a powerful tool later. Furthermore, if possible, ask for a lump sum of cash,

---

[1] "Wedding Budget 101." The Knot, undated, https://www.theknot.com/content/wedding-budget-ways-to-save-money

adjust your budget accordingly, and continue on as you were before.

Why do I say this? Because different parties will have different expectations. Unknown expectations are potential pitfalls. The last thing you want is to have locked in your wedding as a small, intimate affair of 20 only to discover that your mother, on who's largesse you are relying, expects to be able to invite 24 cousins. This needs to be worked out *up front*.

Remember, it's their money, and they may not want to give you money under these conditions. They may say "I'm sorry but if I'm paying I get to invite Uncle Lou." Yet this exercise will still be necessary. Asking for complete control up front is the only way to resolve the issue *now*. It forces them to think through what they desire from your wedding and their money. And you can decide if it's worth it. The importance of this cannot be overstated. Know what you're getting into.

There are myriad traditions around who pays for what in a wedding traditionally. Different family members pay for different things. Some family member may insist on following these traditions, though they seem to be crumbling. If, for example, some family member insists on paying for the rehearsal dinner or the flowers, the best approach is to work out a separate budget line item with them, agree upon the costs, and handle the plans yourself, if you can pull this off. It will be far less stressful in this manner, I assure you.

With a strong budget, discipline on the numbers, discipline with the family, decent negotiating skills and a good bit of luck you will come out of this wedding close to being on budget. For my part, my wedding was about 2 times what I originally planned. I knew it would go over, but because I was lax on these budgeting tactics, and because I procrastinated on several things, it escalated. Had I not been a decent negotiator, things would have been out of control. A wedding is a very large expense for most people. Ask if you can handle it if you accidentally double your budget. If not, follow these steps closely.

A Note On Capitalism

If you read this whole book and find yourself thinking something along the lines of "holy moly this whole ritual is absurd. Insane. I can't believe we're supposed to spend this much money," well, then, my hat is off to you. The average cost of a wedding in the United States is, today, $26,444.[2] I know this because there is a website solely devoted to telling someone the average cost of a wedding in the United States. It's completely insane.

---

[2] See http://www.costofwedding.com/

The same site, however, tells me that most Americans spend less than $10,000 on their wedding. If you remember math class, you remember there is a difference between an average and a median. Slightly more promising.

You're about to read a book that talks about spending vast amounts of money on a single day of your life. It is absurd. Consider not doing it. Consider ditching the whole thing, going to city hall, getting hitched and riding off into the sunset. Seriously. Think about it. There is no shame.

Personally, I have a very conflicted relationship with capitalism. The whole thing seems absurd to me, but it's also the world I live in and I don't feel I have any sort of perfect solution for a better world. In the end, I put all that aside and planned a big wedding. It was important to me to get up there and say to everyone how I felt about my wife. But there were times when we both considered not doing it. Even now, I have mixed feelings. It was a fantastic day, and I will always cherish the memories. People tell me all the time what a great day it was. But when I think of the dollar amount – boy, I sure would like that money back in my bank account.

It's hard to stop the whole crazy process of wedding planning once it's started. Things snowball. Deposits are placed, and they are hard to get back. So.

Take a moment. Ask your partner: do we really want to do this? Do we feel comfortable about spending the money? What if we just... don't?

It's a conversation worth having. And hey. You already bought this book, so what do I care?

Ryan, too, felt the urge to say "screw it" and elope. "Like most couples, my wife and I threatened to elope. Innumerable times. Because planning a wedding is an involved process. It is expensive. And more to the point, it is comprised of a seemingly endless stream of decisions, both large and small that—and here's the big secret—you didn't know even existed in the first place. But like anything you commit to do in life, people will know if you half-ass it. You will know, too. Whole-ass your wedding."

Whole-ass your wedding. *Yes.*

Wedding Planners

You're going to have to decide your approach to hiring a wedding planner. There are essentially three options: go without a professional wedding planner completely, hire one to help plan the whole wedding, or to hire a professional day-of/week-of planner. Each option has its own pros and cons.

Going it Alone

Not hiring a planner at all is swell because you don't have to pay anyone. It is a budget pro move.

Do all the work yourself. The thought of this freaks some people out, but you know what? Let's be frank here for a moment. Wedding planning is not rocket science. It's just event planning. If you keep a cool head, and compartmentalize your emotions and the demands of a million stakeholders, it's not that bad. In the end there are only two people whose opinions matter: you and your future spouse. Everyone else? Take it under advisement. Some you need to listen to, some you don't. Same thing. Don't let the wedding industrial complex fool you, and don't let someone else's freak out threaten your groove. If you want to plan your wedding on your own, you totally can. You got this. It. Is. Not. Rocket. Science.

There are drawbacks to this approach. There's not someone to help you stay on schedule through the process – and staying on schedule is vital. But the biggest risks to not having a professional planner happen the week of your wedding. That's when things get the most intense. If you're going it alone the week of your wedding, you'll need to rely heavily on your groomsmen and friends.

A Full Service Planner

Hiring a professional planner to handle the whole event, however, is a luxury cruise. It's nice. You pay a ton of money. You can amble around and point at things and things magically happen. It is hella expensive, but quite luxurious. In the words of Ferris Bueller, "It is so choice. If you have the means, I strongly recommend picking one up." Write the check, and attend the meetings, with or without your better half. Try not think about how they feel a bit like couples therapy. Remember, you are on a cruise ship. One word of concrete warning, however: everything we've said in the chapter on budget applies, double so, when hiring a professional planner. Cost control takes vigilance when planning a wedding solo, it takes maniacal vigilance when using a professional planner. At least on cruise ships there's not someone following you around going, "Oh, don't you want this slightly-nicer dinner for just 20% more?" all the time. And even if there was, maritime law allows you to hurl them into them into the sea.

That being said a good, budget conscious professional planner can make up a good part of their fee through better negotiating skills, better vendor contacts and detailed scheduling.

The great thing about having a professional wedding planner is their deep access to amazing venues and vendors, that you might not find on your own. This can be incredibly useful. I took a call from a professional wedding planner that had access to a venue I never would have dreamed possible to obtain. Then again, her estimated quote for the whole wedding was ten times what I spent in the end.

Professional planners are also very very helpful for destination weddings, where you may not have any local knowledge at all about neighborhoods, vendors, venues, travel routes, hotels, busy seasons, that sort of thing. I'm the first to say that planning a wedding yourself is not rocket science, but planning a destination wedding, to a popular destination, without a full-service planner, can be logistically intense. Professional planners can provide value here.

The level of participation of your future-spouse is worth considering. If your spouse is going to be super hands-on, and wants to be a part of every decision and weigh every colorway, style, and pattern, having a full-service planner can be useful in order to keep you on time, and to act as a third party intermediary.

Day-of/Week-of

A popular middle-of-the-road option is to hire a professional day-of or week-of planner for your wedding. This is a professional planner who is highly logistics-focused and ensures that everything runs smoothly on the day of the event. They don't help with the venue selection and overall theme. They are there to get things done. Because they're only with you for a couple of weeks at most, they are often much less expensive than an all-inclusive planner. And I find they are much more useful. Or, to be fair, the week of your wedding is when any planner that isn't you is most useful. Because by that point, you're going to be stressed. Guests will be arriving to town. Problems will be arising. And you're going to want to get back into the headspace of romance and being able to enjoy your big day. The last thing you want to be worried about the day before your wedding is the fact that your catering estimate didn't include the serving hardware and you need a new vendor. Let someone else take care of it. My friend Mike concurs.

"We hired a day of wedding planner that would deal with any logistics of getting people to where they needed to be, working with staff, and dealing with the timing. The last thing you ever want to do on your wedding day is deal with people's crap. Make it someone else's job, it's worth every penny." Quite nice.

Professional day-of/week-of planners are also nice because they can do things like run the rehearsal and tell everyone where they need to stand: things that may matter to you but would sound controlling and petty if they come out of the groom's mouth. It gives you someone with third party authority who can be the boss, and you can remain the boss behind the scenes.

One more piece of advice; if you're debating

going for week-of vs. day-of, go for week-of. It will be worth it.

Good professional wedding planners – both full service and week-of/day-of – book up well in advance. Obviously if you've hired a full service planner, who's helping you with the venue and everything else, you will have hired them by the time you do the guest list and save the dates. But even if you're considering hiring a day-of/week-of planner, start looking for them as soon as you've locked down the date.

Let's Talk to Some Planners!

In order to help you make a decision about a wedding planner, as well as to offer some general insight about the tasks that lie ahead of you, I thought it would be useful to talk to two male wedding planners. Jove and Jeremy took some time to answer a few questions about wedding planning.

Interview with a Planner: Jove

Jove Meyer was my week of wedding planner. He was great. He saved my ass on several items. I thought it would make sense to have him chime in on this book, since in many ways he taught me much of what I learned. If you're in the New York area, and you are thinking of hiring a wedding planner for your entire wedding or week-of, I can't recommend Jove highly enough.

Tell me about your history with wedding planning, how you got into it, and what you love about it.

My first wedding was nearly 8 years ago. My best friend Kirstin asked me to plan her wedding and after enjoying every minute of it Jove Meyer Events was born! I love planning and designing weddings as I get to be a part of one of the most special and beautiful days of a couple's life. Weddings are an event of a lifetime and I feel honored that I get to help couples create them! Watching two people express their love and commitment for one another in front of their families and friends is so inspiring, it brings out the inner romantic in me every time!

What are the biggest mistakes most people make when planning a wedding themselves?

Budget, budget budget! Many couples are unaware of what a wedding costs so they overspend in the beginning and then are left with little budget to get the rest of their vendors. I call it "the Porsche syndrome," they want a Porsche but can only afford a Honda. Its crucial to create a budget of all the things you want at the wedding and line item the average cost of them so you have boundaries for your budget and a framework to spend. Some couples fall in love with a venue, book it, then realized they cannot afford much else. Another couple I spoke with booked a band for nearly $14k, of their $30k budget. They have no venue, food, staff, rentals, alcohol and now are trying to get everything else for super cheap.

Have you seen more men planning their weddings lately? Fewer? Any insights or trends you've noticed?

Rick is the first groom I have worked with, in a straight wedding, in all my years of planning. In my experience most straight grooms get involved only in the things that matter to them, the music and or food/alcohol, and let their fiancé handle everything else. Since weddings include a lot of decor and talk about flowers, colors, styles and design most straight grooms are not interested in that. Most straight grooms just want their fiancé to be happy and could care less what flowers are on the table or the color of the napkins, they just want to marry them and celebrate the relationship.

Is the cliché of the man sitting there saying "whatever you want, dear" real?

It is 100% real for men to say "whatever you want, dear!" Many of my meetings sound similar to this, the bride-to-be could talk for hours about flowers, colors, textures and themes meanwhile the groom has a blank face on. In most straight couples it's the bride who has created a Pinterest page, who has bought *The Knot* magazine and who reaches out to me, the wedding planner. When we meet with a florist the groom-to-be generally nods and smiles and says "whatever makes you happy babe" and as much as I try to include grooms in the process, for the most part they are just not interested.

What are your thoughts on day-of/week-of vs. a full service planner? When does it make sense to go full service?

I am a fan of having a planner at a wedding, whether it's just for month-of or full-service a wedding planner is a must, no couple should have to work on their wedding day. Deciding what level of planning is best for a couple is based on a few factors: their budget, free time and organizational skills. Your budget will dictate the level of planning that you can afford. If its on the lower end then you will have to do most of the planning yourself and hire someone for just the month-of. If you have a healthier budget and are busy working full time then hiring a full service planner is the way to go. They will guide you every step of the way and connect you with reliable, talented vendors based on your style, personality and budget.

When you come in as a day-of/week-of planner, what is the number one thing that people have messed up that you have to fix?

When I come in as a day-of coordinator usually the wedding timeline is a mess! The broad timeline is pretty unclear, they think the hair and makeup will take much less time than it really will, same goes for photos, not enough time is allocated. Sometimes they have not yet booked important vendors so we have to move quickly to source, book and manage them.

Describe the biggest wedding planning failure you've seen in your career.

I was working as a day-of coordinator at a venue I love and adore with a very sweet couple! They were on a tight budget and booked a lot of friends and friends of friends as their vendors. I had not heard of 90% of their vendors before but trusted they did their homework and asked all the right questions, I could not have been any more incorrect! They did not hire a traditional full service caterer, they bought food from a few restaurants and had it dropped off, I made sure to let them know they needed to hire a staffing company to set up, serve, bus and break down the event and chefs to heat and prep the food. Day of the wedding, I show up and no one was there. The staffing company, who was also in charge of the bar, showed up nearly two hours late. When they showed up they had no idea what to do, they asked me the most basic questions like "how do I setup a table?" and "which tablecloth goes on which table?" (all the tables were the same). Needless to say I stepped right in and took charge, taught everyone and worked my butt off to get the room set. Thinking this was the biggest hurdle was my mistake. The chefs they hired did not show up, only one of them did and he was over an hour late so there I was playing chef in the kitchen with gloves on plating all of the food and later in the night cutting and serving the wedding cake all while managing the clueless staff. The couple kept asking where I was and it wasn't until they walked into the kitchen that they realized I was wearing many hats for them.

What's the least important aspect of wedding planning people unnecessarily stress about? What's the most important aspect people discount?

I am not sure I think any aspect of wedding planning is not important but I do think that couples over-stress about seating arrangements and spend a lot of time and energy here. Not only on deciding on who sits next to who, and who cannot sit next to who but also how they find out about their seats. While I support assigned seats I encourage couples to make it easier on themselves and assign tables, not seats. Its a little less stress and then you don't need name cards!

One of the most important aspects people discount is the value of a planner. They think that because they have Google and the internet they can plan the wedding all by themselves, but I cannot say enough how having a professional wedding planner by your side for some or all of the planning is crucial.

What advice would you give to a man who is undertaking planning a wedding? Is this advice the same for gay and straight men?

Whether you're gay or straight the advice for men planning their wedding is the same, communicate communicate communicate! Speak to your fiancé and make sure you're on the same page when it comes to size, budget, food and so on. Knowing what your resources are and what your must-haves are before you begin planning is crucial. Being on the same page makes planning so much easier, if a groom goes ahead and books vendors without consulting their finance, male or female, it could be a nightmare. Know what your fiancé wants and what's most important to them, make sure you include it and all will be well.

Interview with a Planner: Jeremy

Jeremy Parades is an old coworker of mine who, as it turns out, used to plan weddings! Quelle coïncidence. He's no longer in the business, so you can't hire him, but he took some time to answer the same questions as Jove and share what he learned through his years helping people plan their weddings.

Tell me about your history with wedding planning, how you got into it, and what you love about it.

Man Nup

I come from a big family so I've always played some part in planning events ever since I was a kid. I started producing events (concerts, festivals, etc.) in college and my first job after school was in experiential marketing, so that's where I got my official event planning chops, so to speak.

I was then asked to plan a few weddings for cousins (a mix of day-of and full-on planning), then friends, and then finally freelance clients. This all happened over the span of five years.

In NYC I run an underground restaurant with my best friend. We started doing more private event design for our regulars at the restaurant and have done a few weddings — sometimes purely catering, sometimes purely floral design — and then one that was full-on for both the service and reception.

My love for cooking, event planning and advertising really comes from the same place. I love to dig and understand what my client is looking for and then work hard to deliver and in surprising ways, over deliver. It's the thrill of bringing a vision to life in ways people never thought possible that I love, whether it be a dish, a design or an experience.

Man Nup

What are the biggest mistakes most people make when planning a wedding themselves?

I think it's odd, but in my experience people dive into "being a wedding planner" and don't first think about the holistic picture. They think they have to dive in and find a venue, schedule a tasting or get a dress, but the reality is they have to decide what kind of experience they want first based on the budget they have.

There are also ways to game the system – a lot of venues come with mandatory vendors and that's almost always going to be more than you want to spend on food or flowers that you don't actually like that much. It might be the best deal or even be a bit easier, but it's always good to weigh a venue that has an open policy for vendors so that you can choose who you want, or even do certain things yourself.

Have you seen more men planning their weddings lately? Fewer? Any insights or trends you've noticed?

Fewer. The trend I see there though is brides giving grooms 1-2 things to own and focus on. Brides tell me, "Talk to him about the cake and the music, but me about everything else." I hear that a lot, actually.

Is the cliché of the man sitting there saying, "Whatever you want, dear" real?

Yes and no. I try and circumvent that with clients (and friends, even more so actually) by asking each person what they feel strongly about for their wedding so I understand what the need to haves are for each, and by doing so I understand what they actually don't care about. That way either person could say whatever you want, and as a planner it's good for me to know what those things are ahead of time.

What are your thoughts on day-of/week-of vs. a full service planner? When does it make sense to go full service?

This is hard for me to answer because everyone I've been a day-of planner for has had a level of event planning experience, so it's never been a problem. I always find a hole here and there of course but I expect that with anyone simply because you're getting a different perspective.

With the number of resources available, I think anyone can plan a wedding. It simply depends on how much time you want to dedicate.

What I actually recommend to people is that you have a consultant that you sit down with at the very beginning of the planning process to help guide your process. They can also assess whether or not a planner's going to help you in the long run. Since I don't do planning full-time, I do this a lot for friends and friends-of-friends, and throughout the process I'll be on-call or even help negotiate with vendors when necessary. I have a few vendors mad at me because I call them on their food costs, oops.

Hm maybe I should consider selling that service, [laughs].

When you come in as a day-of/week-of planner, what is the number one thing that people have messed up that you have to fix?

The biggest mistake I see is people think about their weddings by the tabs in their wedding binders and not as a holistic experience. Whenever I come on as week/day of planner, I pretend I'm a guest and ask step-by-step how I'm getting from one location to the next and what I'm doing upon arrival. In the recent past it's been how to find where to park, how to keep gifts safe or how to get guests from welcome drinks over to the ceremony.

Describe the biggest wedding planning failure you've seen in your career.

I've thought a lot about this and honestly, I haven't seen many! I've actually gotten into the habit of bringing a few event tools with me whenever I go to a wedding – shears for flower arranging, gaff tape, etc. I even started bringing my violin and a few wedding pieces (read: Pachelbel's *Canon*, ugh). I've needed them at every wedding that I've been to in the past couple years. I don't think I averted any failures honestly, but glad to be of service.

What's the least important aspect of wedding planning people unnecessarily stress about? What's the most important aspect people discount?

Everyone stresses about the speeches! When they'll be, where they'll be, how long, how many, etc. Whether or not someone's going to say something embarrassing is a valid thing to stress about, but honestly, the speeches are more of a pleasant moment rather than a memorable one for your guests. The best thing I saw was a friend's wedding (also an event planner) who decided to have them all at the rehearsal dinner and didn't do any at the reception, which was lovely.

I also see people stress about welcome gifts for people in hotels. It's honestly unnecessary, but it's a nice touch. I tell people to try and have fun with them and be as authentic as possible – no need for specialty items, personalized gifts, etc. For one wedding I did, the groom really liked fruit roll-ups and the bride said she always spilled stuff on herself at weddings, so we gave people fruit roll-ups and a tide-to-go pen wrapped in ribbon with a tag that said for before and after. It's meant to be a nice touch, nothing more.

Regarding what aspects people discount, it's again the walkthrough after you've planned every element. It's easy to fall into the pit of thinking about the tabs of your binder or about every individual vendor, but it's important to take a step back and walkthrough your wedding from your guest leaving their door to getting into the hotel at the end of the night.

Man Nup

What advice would you give to a man who is undertaking planning a wedding? Is this advice the same for gay and straight men?

It's different, but in hindsight it shouldn't be. I always ask gay men what wedding traditions are important to them since so many of them are bride/groom focused. It of course doesn't mean they can't partake in every single one (I myself am throwing a bouquet at my wedding and no one's stopping me) but since the frame of reference is heterocentric, it's a good place to start.

I suppose I do ask straight couples the same thing, but it's more of an open question for gay men where I expect them to build a wedding from the ground up, rather than for straight couples the conversation is more about starting with the standard and taking a few elements out.

No matter what, my advice to a man planning their own wedding would be to define what they want vs. what their partner wants, and similarly for their family vs. their partner's family. Identify the conflicts and agree on what to do quickly, then start planning.

Man Nup

Because my experience has been men doing the lesser amount of work compared to their female counterparts, I check in with them often on the project(s) that they're responsible for early and often. Often times, people underestimate how much time it takes to plan things for weddings (unless you know people or know what you're doing – honestly, you could plan a wedding in 3 weeks), I've seen a lot of men start their tasks too late, so I try and avoid that by checking in.

I also hear a lot of men say that the wedding is a chore, but those same men always say they loved the wedding afterwards. So I guess my advice would be to not let the planning and grandeur (no matter how big or small) of the event get in the way of what a wedding is – a celebration of you and your partner coming together. It's supposed to be fun so don't let anything stand in the way of that, least of all your attitude.

Man Nup

Chapter 3: Who Where When

Choosing the Day

You're now ready to choose the big day. This is important. You need to lock down the day and the venue, in tandem, before anything else can happen. You will, of course, need to secure your preferred date with the venue and vice versa. Depending on what's important to you, this may be more complex than it sounds. It'll be more difficult to obtain a venue when you have your mind fixed on one date. With a more flexible date, you will have far more venues for your perusal.

Some people, it should be said, have emotional attachments to specific days. If this is the case, I hope that your emotional attachment is to a day at least 9 months out, as you will have many, many more options. If not, consider postponing the wedding a year. I am serious. This may be unappealing to you, and that is totally okay, but if you don't really care WHEN you get married — because you're happy together *right now*, and getting married is just a piece of paper, man — well, then know that giving yourself ample time to plan will make things much much easier. If the day isn't as important to you, that is good. It will give you more flexibility.

I'm sure you've heard by now that weddings are planned far in advance. You're about to find out just how true that is. Some popular venues are locked down two years in advance, especially on popular days like Saturday (which is also a more expensive day than Fridays and Sundays). It is completely crazy. It'll make you wonder who these people are, right before you, maybe, become one of them. Here are some things to consider when choosing the day.

Popular venues fill up on Saturdays about a year in advance. By six months in advance, alternative popular days such as Fridays and Sundays are usually full in popular venues, and less popular venues are pretty full up as well. Also by six months out, less convenient time slots in venues such as hotels in Vegas that handle multiple ceremonies per day are starting to fill up. You can pretty much book a weekday wedding, barring holidays, right up until a month or two before the ceremony, but your guests will hate you for it. If you're a cabal of circus performers or comic book artists with no family, however, this may be just the thing for you.

You'll want to double-check the day you finally choose. Look the date up on Wikipedia. (For you stoners out there, I just want to give you a heads up that 4/20 is also Hitler's birthday, so, yeah.) Check it against your friend's birthdays. Holidays are expensive, especially Valentine's day. During the December holidays, many good venues are booked up by company holiday parties, and you will need to book well in advance. Expect extra costs with these as well. If you are considering doing your wedding on a three day weekend, god help us all. Especially Columbus Day. We *need* that. No, I kid. But do be aware that some people simply won't show up – they value their three day weekends too highly. Check with your closest friends and loved ones about their feelings on your wedding taking up one of their holidays. Finally, be aware of holidays that are holidays for you, but not for others. In Massachusetts, I saw a lot of Patriots' day weddings – a three-day holiday for us in the state, but not for anyone visiting from afar.

This date is going to be your anniversary for (hopefully) the rest of your life. Consider where in the year it falls. Consider both of your birthdays, the birthdays of your loved ones, other major holidays. If you have an innate fear of elves and reindeer, perhaps a Christmas-time wedding is not for you. Consider a destination wedding in the summer, someplace hot. There will be less Santa's Workshops to maneuver, and no one is going to make you touch an old-timey steel and wood sled. These things don't matter to some people, but they may matter to you. Better to know what you're getting into at this early juncture, because it will prove very difficult to move the date once things get rolling.

Then there's scheduling the time of day. You don't need to decide this right away if you have booked your venue for the whole evening, and you can get your save the date cards out without knowing the exact time. For our part, our wedding and reception were in one location, and we had that location the whole night, so we didn't decide the exact time until a month or two before the wedding. Other venues, however (especially specialized wedding chapels in Vegas, for example), serve several weddings at a time, and you will need to decide the time in advance. This will need to dovetail with the time for any other venues you may need to book, mainly the venue for the reception.

This is not to say its impossible to plan a wedding at the last minute – it's more difficult, and fewer options are available, but it's doable. This might not be a problem if you and your beloved are super into gutter weddings. Or a lovely event in a parking lot. Many of my friends and relatives have been married in town hall, there's nothing wrong with this. There's a lot that's right with this. But just know that if you intend to do a Proper Regular Big Fancy Wedding, every day that you lose to the relentless ticking time bomb of a calendar will be payed for by money, tears, or blood. Lots of blood.

My friend Richard, who planned his wedding on a budget and in a hurry, is reassuring when it comes to doing things last minute. "When you're planning a wedding in less than ten weeks you'll save a lot of money. Wedding vendors are sometimes booked nine months to two years in advance, so if you plan on doing one in a little over *two months* there is a good chance that if they aren't already booked, there isn't anyone crazy enough to book in a shorter period of time. So you're basically crazy like a fox and you can get a discounted rate." *No fear.*

There's another far more important factor to consider when deciding how far in advance to plan your wedding: your guests. Now you may be, like me, someone who enjoys jetting off to the far corners of the world at a moment's notice. You may be completely comfortable with booking a plane ticket on a Thursday for Friday. What I have learned in planning a wedding, however, is that many people plan things far, far in advance. Because of a mix-up with our first choice of venues (long story, grumble grumble), we ended up not being able to lock down the venue for our wedding, and thus the date, until about eight months before the wedding. This means we got the save-the-date cards out a mere eight months (gasp!) before the wedding. By that point, four or five of our guests had already made plans that could not be moved (including two other weddings that were more proactively planned than ours).

Some people like to plan in advance. There are some life events that are planned a year or more out – having children, sabbaticals, other weddings, career or housing moves – and people like to be able to plan around other important events, such as your wedding. I've also found that the elderly like to plan trips far more in advance than the young. You do, after all, want them to show up.

Finding a Venue

So now we have to choose our venue. Or venues. For that is the first big decision. Are you going to have a separate venue for the ceremony and the reception? Here are the two broad approaches: You choose the specific date, and find a venue that works, or vice versa. Either is doable. If you have two venues, you will have to book them both on the same day. And to reiterate: the best venues book early. Start this in advance. Until you've locked down the venue and the date, you can't start inviting people.

When I wrote my "things most important to me about my wedding" list, the number one most important thing to me was that the ceremony and the reception were in the same place. I hate moving around. I wanted to settle into one place for the evening, and have a nice time. I didn't want to move. It also cut down on the transportation costs, as I didn't have to rent additional transportation (even better, I picked a venue right by my house so we could walk to the wedding!) It was great. I strongly recommend it. I also wanted my wedding to go late. So we did the whole thing in a nightclub, that could stay open until 4 AM. I also loved that. Personally, as a man that likes to hang out with his friends late at night, I find that many wedding receptions and venues close down early. Then you gotta go find a third place to keep on hanging out, and that can be a hassle. Your opinions may well vary, however. You might find yourself exhausted after 8 hours of wedding festivities, and ready to go to bed. Let your guests sort out their own continued merriment. This is totally valid as well.

Many people, however, want to get married in a church, and for many people it's hard to have a big party in a church. Thus two venues are unavoidable. That's okay. To each his own.

Now, we should say that choosing your venue, you should have in mind a broad number of people who you think are coming to your wedding. A good policy is to make a quick first-pass guest list and see broadly how many people you can think of off the top of your head. This will give you a rough idea. Conversely, you can choose the venue and let the venue size dictate the guest list size, since you can, obviously, only invite as many people as will fit in the venue. Sort of. More on that later. The point here is that it's important to look for venues that house broadly the right number of people.

Some tips:

Morning and afternoon weddings are cheaper. If you want my opinion, they are cheaper because they are less fun. But hey, that's just me. If you do a morning wedding, there can be a nice break where people can go and nap before an evening reception and dinner. It's harder to book evening weddings in a church, but it is possible. Churches tend to do several weddings a day, and it's rather difficult to do a church wedding at the time the church is having a service (duh). I'm not a religious man, but I suspect if you are, you know the requirements your faith will place upon you in being allowed to use their house of worship for your ceremony. Plan in advance.

Traffic is a thing. Some times of day (especially if you're going for a Friday wedding) have more traffic in the big cities, and you should factor it in.

If you are having an outside wedding, think about the weather. Check the seasonal weather and make sure that it's unlikely to rain in this locale at this time of year (duh). Plan for rain anyway, by having a tent or a backup venue. For these reasons, outdoor weddings can be more expensive – though there are some venues that allow you to book the venue and choose the exact location of the ceremony on the day of. That's nice of them. Outdoor weddings. I couldn't do it. I would be so stressed out. I've been to some that poured down rain. I've been to some that were freezing. I'm too much of a control freak, myself. This, obviously, is less of a risk in, say, Vegas, than New England.

Ryan tells us of a fun tax loophole for weddings in public parks and the like. "Certain public venues, like parks, botanical gardens, and observatories, will allow you claim some fees as tax-deductible, charitable contributions on your return, which is nice for you and good for them, since most city and state parks are grossly underfunded anyway. Plus, they're generally nice places to host an outdoor wedding. Picture the dappled afternoon sun filtered through crimson maple leaves blown gently by a fresh, lakeside breeze, as the birds punctuate your wedding vows with their melodious ebullience. You helped conserve that shit with your venue cash, John Muir!"

There are a host of logistical puzzles you'll need to solve with these public venues, since they won't have many of the services you'd expect from strictly events-oriented shops, but if that's your game, you might shave a few bucks off your taxes by doing a little bit of research on what your town has to offer.

Unsurprisingly, to choose a venue you have to go visit some venues. I went to about four. You can do a ton of research online – there are some seriously great sites for event venue selection, especially in larger cities – but eventually you're going to have to visit. I found this really fun. You get to see lots of interesting spaces, and go back stage, feel like a rock star or a priest or what have you.

The usual "groom with a wedding vendor" situation applies here – they'll be a bit confused you're not a woman, and they'll probably persevere in trying to up-sell you.

When it comes to booking and holding a venue for your event. there's this whole complex world of first and second holds, and backup venues. A queue of bookings, prioritized: if the first hold backs out, the slot goes to the second hold. If you have your heart set on a venue, this might be a path for you. You can book a backup venue, and take the second hold on your favorite venue, and cross your fingers that the original hold cancels. You can also book, say, an alternate time – the afternoon slot, for example, with a second hold on your coveted evening slot. As long as you definitively have one venue locked down, you can get the save the date cards out – just don't put the exact time and venue on the save the date card.

Lock down your venue with a deposit. Get a contract. Make sure they can't back out on you. The last thing you need is to tell a bunch of people to come to a certain town on a certain date and not have anywhere to throw the shindig.

The Guest List

Once your venue is chosen, you know the maximum number of people who can come to your wedding. Venues have capacities, and you can't exceed the capacity.

Time to work up a guest list.

Draw up a draft of the list. Use something like Google Docs. Let you and your spouse take a pass, adding everyone that you both want at the wedding. If your family is paying, and it's understood that they get to invite some people, then include them in this process. And even if they're not, Richard offers some great tactical advice regarding family and your parents: "Invite your parents friends because they're the ones that are going to give you the most amount of money, even if they don't show up." Richard is very wise. Shrewd, but wise.

The first pass is the easy one. Just do it. Ryan

notes that "my wife and I covered our living room with post-it notes one sunny Sunday, one for each guest, and we arrived at a first draft in a surprisingly short time. When you're not worried about the fine details on the first go-round, you can actually move pretty quickly."

The odds are that this first pass will be much longer than you have room for in the venue. If this is the case, you're going to need to cut some people.

Whittling down the list will take time, patience, negotiation and compromise. Ryan notes that "We spent far more time on the revisions than the initial arrangement, so a format that allows you to move people around easily will make your life so much easier. Post-it notes are cheap. Buy many, and dive in head-first." There will be times you'll think you couldn't possibly cut anyone else. I promise, though, through all of this, in the end, you will still be surrounded by loved ones and it will be a great night. Consider cutting entire groups from the invite list, such as coworkers or college friends. No one will notice an absence because the others won't be there either. Take the number of guests the venue will fit, and divide the list out. If the venue is 200 people, and you, your spouse and your mom are involved, give 75 spots each to you and your spouse, and 50 to your mom, for example. Another tactic is for both of you to go through and mark anyone that one of you absolutely don't want at the wedding. Some couples make an agreement in advance that each has veto power. Others negotiate ("you can invite that bore Sally if I can invite Jim even though you think he's a tool.") Another popular tactic is to mark everyone you haven't seen in a year, although personally I find that rather painful as I often miss them the most.

Also remember that some of these people may make it back in the mix as the RSVPs come in. The number is rough, and the sooner the wedding is, the more people won't be able to show up, but a decline rate of somewhere in the 10-25% range is realistic.

So here's how it goes: you invite in waves. Invite wave one – the people you most want to come. Set an RSVP deadline. See how many "no's" you get. Don't assume if someone didn't answer they are not coming. You'll have to nag them. But any "no" you get does mean that's one less person not coming, and one more person you can invite. When you get a batch of "no's," invite another wave of people. You might go through this process a couple of times. This can seem a little like favoritism, and hey, it probably is. People sometimes know they're on the B list, but that's up to them to decide if they want to go or not. And, again, the earlier you do the whole thing, the less likely it is that people feel that way. Someone gets an invite 8 months before a wedding vs 12? They don't feel so B list. They get an invite 3 weeks before? B list.

Venue size and number of friends is a factor in giving guests the ability to bring someone along with them (known as "plus ones"). But there are other factors. It's always struck me as a little odd that if I'm married, I automatically get a plus one to a wedding, but if I have a long term partner and we're not married, or if I'm single, then I do not get a plus one. This is odd, because going to a wedding solo can be a little daunting, and it's good to have backup. Then again, you may not want a bunch of strangers at your wedding. My revelation on this while planning my wedding is that no one ever knows everyone at their wedding, there are always going to be some people you don't know. Even without the +1 situation, your spouse may have a long lost cousin, a high school friend you've never met, what have you. A plus one for your single friend isn't going to ruin the situation – odds are you're already not going to know everyone. Unless your wedding is like 6 people. It's best not to worry too much about it. We want to make our guests feel comfortable. This is what we did: if someone was married or in a long term relationship, we invited them and their partner by name. If we were good friends with both people in the couple before they got married, we invited them as individuals. Anyone single we gave a plus one. The more the merrier, we figured. Now, this can get expensive, and it might not be an option for you. That's okay. I advise fairness and consistency. People are going to notice if you dole out plus ones to some people and not others without a good reason.

I should also say that in the eight months between when our save the date cards went out and the wedding, five couples broke up. If you've planned your invites and +1's right, then this doesn't have to be an emergency – this is why we invited both friends separately even if they were in a couple. Because even if they broke up, we wanted to make them both feel welcome. Whereas if someone was dating a stranger, we would simply add them to their spouse's invitation.

Save the Date

Since it is one of the first visual pieces you'll need to create, you can use a save the date card as the project that defines the look and feel of the whole event. This is a card that you send to all of your potential wedding guests well in advance of the wedding, to let them know they are invited, and they should, well, save the date on their calendar. You should be sending this out as soon as you have your date, venue and guest list locked down.

Think about the charter – or vision – of the wedding in terms of graphic design. You're going to need to find a graphic designer who can help you turn your vision into something graphic. You may have a friend in mind. It may be someone you know. We bring this up now because you are going to want to find this vendor early. One of the things that makes a wedding look like a seriously pro affair is quality, consistent graphic design: from the invitations to the place cards to the wedding program and any signage. And in order for the whole affair to feel cohesive – as if it's really going for some specific feel – you need that look and feel to follow from the wedding's vision.

What this means is that when you're selecting a graphic designer for the save the date cards, you are, in reality, selecting a graphic designer for your entire wedding. For this reason, don't use some design-a-card service from a print shop or something like that. It's becoming increasingly acceptable to use online services for save the date cards. We'll talk about online services later, and you should feel free to use them for all but the most formal weddings. Even when using an online service, it's still a good idea to use the occasion as a launching pad for your design vision. Try not to simply use a default template. Sit down with the designer you're engaging and tell them that this first piece is going to be the first statement of a more broad look and feel, and you're looking for someone to design all of the pieces for the wedding.

Man Nup

Share your Pinterest board with them. We'll get into the individual components that need designing later, but the reason we bring this up now is important: the design should flow from the vision. Everything should be coherent.

Man Nup

Chapter 4: Logistics

Making a Wedding Day Itinerary

You're going to want to make a minute-by-minute itinerary of your big day. Do it in something like Google Docs. Actually, the other day I was talking to this guy who was going to make a startup just around doing wedding itineraries. It was a great idea. Hopefully by now he's made that company, and if not, you should totally go start that company. The first time I got one of these (I was acting as a groomsman) I thought the bride was going a little bridezilla and being overly-obsessive, but I came around pretty quickly. It's actually super helpful for everyone involved. And if there's one day it's annoying having people be late, it's your wedding day (I'm looking at you, guy who was supposed to be there early to play our processional music).

Start working on this itinerary early – like a couple months in advance. You're going to be working it and re-working it several times, as you remember things and get dates and times from various vendors. If you have a week-of planner, this is something they can take over for the last week before the wedding, but trust me they will love you for having started it. Also make a worksheet of everyone's name, role, phone number and email: the wedding party, relatives, and all vendors. Everyone should get a copy of the itinerary. You gotta keep everyone organized.

One thing you'll notice as you do this is that your hopes of sleeping in before the big day are going to be more or less dashed – doubly so if you've gone and done something daring like have an afternoon wedding. There's a *lot* to do before the ceremony. Women need to get their hair and make up done and this takes time – more so if you only have one stylist and one makeup artist. People need to tie bow ties and put on boutonnieres and corsages. Lots of people need to shower, bathrooms may be at a premium. Trust me. Getting to sleep in will be hard. Build up a sleep surplus in the few days in advance of your wedding. Schedule it.

Finding Vendors

Throughout this book, we will talk about many vendors. You will need to hire many, many people. Most wedding books spend inordinate amounts of time talking about where to find good vendors. But the answer is basically the same for all of them: look on the internet, ask your friends, and ask the people at the venue, once you have one. If you have a planner, this is a huge, huge skill for them. You can use wedding sites on the internet, local search sites such as Yelp and Foursquare or Google. It's my view that the wedding world is so hyper-competitive that there are many good vendors out there. Read the ratings on rating sites. Finding vendors through friends is obviously better than Google. Be slightly more vigilant on contract terms and money when investigating recommendations from your venue, but don't discount them outright. They know the space, they know what works, and they tend to be very effective. My venue recommended a florist and an equipment rental company and they were both great.

When negotiating with vendors, bear in mind the 30% below budget rule. Again, never, ever, state your real budget. Give them a wide range, but keep it on the low side. If you can swing it, force them to give you an initial bid without you giving a budget (this works better for the food, beverage, equipment rental, entertainment and photography vendors than it does for, say, the flowers). Always try and get estimates from 2-3 vendors, minimum. Have a backup. Do not be afraid to negotiate. Some of us find negotiation a great time, some are terrified of it, but you will need to get the hang of it. If a vendor's too expensive, say so outright. Don't be afraid to make a counter offer. Richard reinforces the value of negotiation. "All wedding vendors have flexible rates. From the caterers, to the florists, DJ's, photographers, you should never pay full price for anything. Even if you shave only 10% from every vendor it all adds up to significant savings in the end."

We'll talk about planning timing in a bit, but this tends to work when you are very early – as in locking things in before other people – or very late – as in it's a week before, they don't have a gig, some money is better than none. The very late approach is fraught with peril. Many quality vendors are booked months in advance, or more. I ran into this problem when I forgot to book a photographer, and all the good ones I wanted were booked up. I eventually found a great one through a recommendation from one of the photographers I *couldn't* get.

If the vendor you've selected hasn't been in business for a long time or isn't highly reputable, take care to either book a backup vendor or, at the very least, keep your initial deposit to a minimum. I've known people whose vendors have gone out of business between when they booked and their wedding date, taking the couple's deposit with them. If it's a big wedding, an expensive dinner, or you're tight on funds, this is obviously an even worse blow. Consider the reputation of the vendor when making a final decision. Despite the variation of bid amounts, extremely low bids from relatively new establishments should be treated with some measure of skepticism.

Your wedding could potentially have dozens of people working it. Venue employees, caterers, bartenders, servers, food prep personnel, people from the rental equipment company, decorators, florists, photographers. Two things to note here:

First, never assume any bid from any vendor includes actual people on site unless it explicitly says it does. For example, I thought my cupcake bid came with someone to lay out all the cupcakes when they arrived. No such luck. We had to rapidly negotiate with other vendors present to handle the task.

This leads to our second point. When working your timeline, make a column for who or which team is responsible for the task and how many people will be required to do it. This can be a very complex task, and is a large part of what a good wedding planner does that makes them so expensive. For example, if after the ceremony you need chairs cleared away so that later on the same space may be used as the dance floor, you need to identify exactly who will do this and make sure they know this and agree to it. Once your timeline – with responsibilities – is in draft form, make sure you share it with every vendor, go through it line by line, and be sure they are aware of their responsibilities. Some vendors will balk, claiming some of the tasks you have assigned to them are not theirs.

You will need to negotiate a different fee, find another team to do it, or hire a new batch of people. I find the place this is most risky is with an equipment rental company that does not provide personnel to handle the equipment. These risks will be commensurately less if you are using an all-in-one vendor such as a hotel for your whole shindig.

For some smaller, more charming or indie weddings, using friends can add a charming touch. Caveats apply to working with friends, however. Be sensitive to the amount of work you are asking them to do. Consider paying them. Don't put anyone out. Remember that some people just want to enjoy the wedding. When using friends to help with things, consider not putting all of one task on a single friend. That being said, I went to one wedding where the bride worked in event management and while the entire staff were not necessarily her close friends, they were all friends and acquaintances, and thus quite charming. They enjoyed what they did for a living, were kind, and fun, and did a spectacular job. It was a splendid time.

Tipping

Every single person working your wedding needs to be tipped. Plan for this. Add it into your budget when you are doing the original planning. Ap-

propriate tip amounts can vary widely by type of service offered, geography, and even time of year. If you
have a wedding planner, they will know the local best
practices. If not, consult the Internet, or, even better,
talk to the people providing the services. Yes, asking
the person booking the catering might be a bit of a
conflict of interest, but they will generally be trust-
worthy and besides, it's not like they're the ones getting the tips. You can also ask multiple vendors their
opinions during the vendor selection process in order
to make sure no one person is yanking your chain.

Personally, I quite enjoy handing out tips at
the end of a party. It's a fun little opportunity to feel
like Santa Claus. Practically speaking, however, it's
probably more logistically feasible to have your wedding planner or, failing their existence, your best man
to handle the duties. Cash is preferable. Don't be like
Aunt Mabel and hand out Applebee's gift cards. Give
the best man or wedding planner sealed envelopes
with names marked on them. If you're feeling especially vulnerable to embezzlement because, say, your
best man is also a pirate, you can discretely mention
to each of the vendor managers that your best man
is handling the tips and to come bug you if there's a
problem.

And hey – don't be cheap. I liberally tipped at
my wedding, and virtually every time I walk by the

venue (it's just down the street from my house), the door man *who I never even met the night of my wedding* lets me walk right in and see the show. Saw Godspeed You! Black Emperor there last month.

Rentals

You're going to need to rent a LOT of shit. It's kind of amazing. Basically, your rule of thumb should be to assume that no one is providing anything, at all, ever, beyond exactly what they say they are. If you are buying, just hypothetically, 500 cupcakes for your wedding, they are going to show up in boxes, with absolutely zero way to display them. No one will bother to tell you you might need to rent some really nice pastry display stands. You know, just hypothetically. Your caterers are bringing food, but unless they explicitly say otherwise, they are probably not bringing serving hardware, tables, tablecloths, or anything else. They're almost certainly not bringing plates and silverware. Everything will need to be rented. All-in-one firms, such as hotels usually offer rental equipment in their comprehensive bid. However, even in these situations, these often come from a third party, and you should explicitly ask what's included and what's not.

If you have a wedding planner, they will know this, and they will have a few good rental places in mind. These places are amazing. They are vast warehouses with innumerable copies of every item under the sun: thousands of knives, forks, chargers, small round high tables, small round low tables, long tables, chairs of infinite variety, plates, serving tongs. It goes on forever. Rental places are really magical. Have you seen Indiana Jones and the Raiders of the Lost Ark? It's like that warehouse where they stash the ark, but with way less haunted relics and way more slightly stained baby booster seats.

But if you don't have a wedding planner, these places are going to be entirely new to you. You're going to need to find a good one. Google's your friend, as per usual. Make a note of places that specialize in weddings. Remember: for every vendor you talk to, ask what equipment they provide and do not provide. Ask your venue if it provides chairs, tables, tablecloths – anything you can think of. And no, they very well may not. Do this for your caterer. Make an ongoing list.

You'll also need to budget a lot for your rentals. We alluded to this in the budgeting chapter, but rentals can be a significant expense. You can tweak and modify your list – exact numbers of items, adding or taking out a thing here or there – right up until the day before your wedding, but you need a rental vendor selected, with a contract signed, maybe a month in advance.

Hospitality Logistics

Unless your wedding is next door to your house (ours was!) you may want to consider a hotel room for your wedding night and perhaps the night before. This is obviously true if you are involved in a destination wedding, but it may be useful for other reasons as well: if your wedding or reception takes place in a hotel, why not stay there? This is also convenient if all of your wedding party is staying in the same hotel, as you will all have a centralized place to prepare – this is something which you're gonna need. If you have roommates and you want some privacy, consider a hotel. A couple words on this matter: first, you're going to have to bring a LOT of stuff to your hotel from your house. For this reason its a good idea to stay in the hotel the night before, bringing everything over the day before your wedding. Also be sure to book a late checkout. Who wants to wake up early the day after their wedding? Finally, while it's right and proper you would want to get a luxury suite for your wedding, do consider also springing for an additional one for the maid of honor and perhaps the best man as well, so there is somewhere to prepare for your wedding that isn't in your hotel room. Some people may find it fun to have a drunk bridesmaid pop in at 3 in the morning looking for her shoes, but some may appreciate the additional privacy a separate suite for prep can provide.

Lodging For Your Guests

Many hotels will provide hotel blocks for wedding guests. This allows you to get a bulk rate discount, making the hotel a little bit cheaper for everyone (though honestly, not much). It's good to get a wedding block at a hotel, especially if your wedding is in a small town where there are only one or two hotels. Do think about the price – by definition those staying in a hotel are traveling, so the wedding is already something of an expense for them. If your only hotel block is in a five star luxury hotel, some will not be able to afford it.

That being said I find that, in cities, a lower and lower percentage of the total number of wedding guests actually stay at the hotel you have set aside for the wedding block. If you're in the country and there are fewer places to stay, it still seems to be the de facto option. Either way, the wedding party should stay there, so you're all in one place for preparation. The family, too, tends to stick to the "official" hotel. But many other wedding guests don't stay at the "official" hotel for a variety of reasons – chiefly to save money but also because they want something more luxurious or funky. This is no big deal, really.

One thing to look out for: the distribution of gift bags for the wedding guests. Hotels with wedding blocks often also offer the service of handing out a bag of "stuff" to each guest as they check in. This may be a small gift, an itinerary for the weekend or perhaps a hangover kit. These are very nice, but don't count too much on relying on it as a surefire means of distributing information, as many people will never receive them if they are staying elsewhere. Consider alternative means of passing this stuff out – an email for the info, and a gift bag as people leave the ceremony, or at the night-before event for example.

Online House Rentals

In touristy destinations and large cities, I find that more and more guests are turning to Airbnb and other online room and house rental tools to find affordable, or just generally more homey, lodgings. This is a good thing. Often people can find something that suits their specific needs – if, for example, they have a new baby and need more privacy. It can also be fun to have 3 or 4 different groups of wedding guests go in on rental houses together. This is going to happen anyway, so you may as well try and assist by offering some sort of centralized means for people getting in touch with each other about lodging – perhaps by email or a Facebook group. Staying for a few days with a bunch of friends at a rental house in a nice destination can be a lovely experience. Some couples choose to take this route themselves! Hotels. Thing of the past, amirite?

However: a word of warning. Airbnb and its ilk are often not as regulated as hotels. They may not even be legal. In many cities in America, a battle is being waged regarding the legality, licensing and taxing of owner-rented lodging. *Just because a property is on the site, doesn't mean it's legal.* Hotels have stringent safety regulations for a reason. While individual guests may choose to rent an Airnbnb property, beware of handling any group bookings for liability reasons.

Transportation

When it comes to transportation, think through how you and your better half – along with the wedding party – will get to the ceremony, to the reception, and back to the hotel. For that matter, what about the guests? Is your wedding out of the way? In the woods? On the moon? Some places require assisted transportation. Think about alcohol: do you want your guests to drink and drive?

There are myriad options here, depending on whether you're in a city or the country or whether the ceremony is somewhere easily accessible by public transportation. At the very least you'll need to make sure you and the wedding party have a means to get around for the evening – often this means limousine or shuttle bus rental. If your wedding involves a lot of drinking and isn't at the hotel, it might be good to help think through how the wedding guests will get to and from the wedding. I went to a farm wedding once, for example, that was in a town with no cabs, and very far from our hotel. Not an easy place to get to and from. I passed out in a barn and walked home early in the morning. I am not kidding. Hopefully no one noticed. Think this through. Include the details in your wedding itinerary for the wedding party.

Some people like to do wacky stuff – I recently spotted a bunch of people piling onto one of those silly tourist trollies in Chicago headed off to a wedding. These can be fun. Why not. And who doesn't love a school bus back from the reception to the hotel? And if you can work a train ride into your festivities, my hat goes off to you.

The usual vendor selection advice applies. I would apply extra attention on the limo rental, however. Some limos are pretty run down. You want something really nice. A posse of nice luxury Town Cars or Escalades might be more stylish than a run down stretch limo.

Chapter 5: Food and Drink

Dinner

The food and drink for your wedding can be one of, if not the largest, expense of your wedding. Both can be monstrously expensive. Take care in your initial planning and budgeting to allocate enough money for food and drink – they will probably be 40% of your total expenses, including rentals (more on rentals later).

Let's walk through the details.

Dinner is hella expensive. Broadly speaking, a buffet dinner is less expensive than a served dinner. In both cases, however, you're essentially paying by the person.

Most people have opinions about the type of food you are serving – that is right and proper. Having very specific opinions about the exact restaurant from which you obtain your food, however, can cause costs to spiral. Choosing a cuisine is less expensive than choosing a restaurant. It also makes it easier to book a food vendor after you've booked a venue. If you want a specific restaurant, it's important to co-ordinate with them on choosing the date of your big event, to ensure they are available.

There may be some desire to save money by having someone cook your wedding dinner – say, a friend. Avoid this. It's monstrously stressful, and unless they are pros, you'll be worried till the bitter end that things aren't going to work out. Plus, unless this said friend owes you a bunch of money or something, you're going to feel like a heel for not paying them for their efforts, and then you'll be getting into expensive territory regardless. Professional restaurants can buy their ingredients for less money than your friend going to the grocery store. Besides, either way, a large chunk of the cost of dinner at a wedding is the service personnel, which in either case, you're going to have to pay. Unless, like, the Fraternal Brotherhood of Caterers in your hometown owes you a giant favor because you, like, saved their building from a fire or something. In which case, go for it. Also, do you really want half your friends working your wedding? It's weird. Best to pay professionals, and if you're tight on funds, scale back from served to buffet, or look for cheaper restaurants.

Worst case, scale back the number of the guests at your wedding. This is not a joke. Back in your original planning, you should be deciding how many people you can have at the wedding based on how many people you can afford to feed. It is the biggest per-person expense, and should be considered at all times.

In choosing a restaurant, as with everything wedding related, lock in your vendor early. Up to a year early. The good ones book up. The cheap ones book up quicker still.

As we've said, try not to get hooked on one specific restaurant. Being into a specific cuisine is easier. Whip up a simple Request for a Proposal (RFP) and send it off to 5-10 restaurants in your area that you like that serve that cuisine. Specify the date, the number of people, the time, whether it's buffet or served (or you want bids for both) and whether or not you want them to include the cost of equipment rentals (or get bids with both). Send it out, and get back the bids.

The first thing you'll notice is that there is a wide range of prices in the bids. This is normal. You'll feel a lot better about spending $7,000 on your food when three of the other bids were over $10,000. This is why it's so important to get multiple bids. Once you've chosen one you like, don't hesitate to negotiate further. These bids are often highly flexible.

Some venues insist on using their catering service. This is distinct from venues that will supply you a list of approved, or recommended caterers. If venues provide such a list, simply work them into your potential bidders. If a venue requires you work with a specific set of caterers, or with only the venue itself as a carter, then obviously this decision needs to be made in tandem with your venue selection. A combination venue-catering situation can definitely be cheaper than booking the two separately, and eliminates scheduling/availability concerns. However, it can also be more expensive, and it's possible the food options will limit you in a way you do not like. Pay attention and do the math.

Look for opportunities, especially if you know some great up and comer. Mike did this to stellar results. I was there. God, that food was good. "Food was important to us so we hired a catering company to do logistics like servers and flatware but wanted to bring in our own chef. I asked this up and coming chef to cater our wedding because we had eaten at his popup restaurant and it was fantastic. Two weeks after he agreed to do it he received 3 Michelin stars and 4 NY Times stars. He was locked in for cheap and blew everyone away at the reception."

In delivering the bids, the vendors will usually send along a sample menu. You can make tweaks and adjustments, but generally it's best to do this once you've selected your specific vendor.

Regarding dietary restrictions, you'll know your friends, and so you will have a good idea how important this is, but even the most staid wedding entourage has one or two vegetarians. There are two effective approaches here: when serving buffet style, all you really need to do is make sure there are one or two good vegan and gluten free items, label them, and people can self select.

Alternatively, you can do an exact count, preferably along with your RSVP card, and let your caterer know the exact numbers, and have servers serve accordingly. This is logistically more complex, and expensive, but it's a nice, classy touch people appreciate. Virtually every wedding caterer in the U.S. will accommodate these approaches.

A Note On Imposing Your Own Values

We occasionally come across weddings that seek to impose their own values on the guests, by way of serving or not serving specific food or drink. We've seen vegan weddings, alcohol free weddings, you name it. I used the word "impose," because personally, I like a good cocktail at a wedding and as a guest I might get a little bit sad if there aren't any. But you know what? It's your big day, and if you don't want a bunch of dead animals being served on your big day – or a bunch of drunks – I say more power to you. That is your right.

What I think is a good compromise is to let people know in advance. Something on the invitation is probably best, that says "please be aware we have chosen to celebrate our big day without alcohol. Therefore this will be a booze-free wedding. We wanted to warn you. We hope that's okay but if it makes you feel uncomfortable, we understand." Or words to that effect. I would never skip a good friends wedding because there wasn't booze, but I'd be much happier knowing the situation going in. Win win!

Rehearsal Dinner

Many of the basic principles in selecting your reception dinner vendor apply to your rehearsal dinner. Obviously, however, the food and the venue are one in the same. Best practices still include looking at several potential places, focusing on a cuisine (or location, or ambiance) rather than a specific vendor, and setting a per person budget. Be sure to negotiate with the restaurant, select your location early, and focus on specific menu selection and tweaking once you have narrowed things down to a single venue. The same warnings about new or shady venues apply.

Because rehearsal dinners tend to be smaller, you can usually afford a higher per-guest amount, and the odds are much better that you can have the meal served, restaurant style, rather than buffet style. Many rehearsal dinners are prix fixe, with a set menu. The restaurant will work with you on the menu.

Make sure to have either vegetarian/vegan/gluten free options. Or, better yet, since the numbers are small, simply ask everyone whether anyone has any dietary restrictions, and provide an exact count to the restaurant. Most restaurants will comply.

The Cake

The wedding cake. Hoo boy. For your average dude reading this book not up to speed on wedding culture, here's the thing about wedding cakes. They actually kinda taste like cardboard crap. Usually. Things are getting better – god, you should have tasted wedding cakes in the eighties. So bad. You may have experienced this while attending past weddings. Indeed I've noticed at most weddings that half or more of the guests don't even bother eating the wedding cake. With good reason. Traditional wedding cakes are built for beauty, not deliciousness.

If you were to pick up a traditional wedding planning book, right here would be this whole elaborate section outlining different kinds of frostings -er, sorry, icings. These include fondant (gross), butter cream (gross) and whipped cream (probably gross). It would talk about seasonal considerations (pumpkin or carrot spice in the winter, blah blah blah). It would have a whole section, if not chapter, on cake toppers (a couple of figurines on the top of your cake, in case you are wondering). Like I said before, if you care about a traditional wedding, read a traditional wedding planning book for details on this stuff.

Some practical tips include cost: figure $1.50 to $12 a person, based on how psychotic you are. Also consider a smaller cake if you have other desserts. Also consider a very small wedding cake for the whole couple-cutting-the-cake ritual and additional, cheaper, sheet cakes for the masses. Usual vendor guidelines apply in finding a quality vendor, and the caveats about leaving this to friends. If you doubt me, Google "wedding cake disasters."

Consider chucking the cake completely. We used cupcakes, and it was stupendous. This also allowed us to have vegan and gluten-free options – a must-have here in Williamsburg, Brooklyn. I went to a wedding recently in Chicago that had a cookie bar and it was glorious. Also, cupcakes/cookies make better leftovers if all of them aren't consumed at the wedding. Planning an exact amount of pieces of cakes or cupcakes is very hard. Some people have more than one piece, some people have none. I find 0.75 pieces/cupcakes per guest is a good coefficient.

Groom Cake

A full 18% of the weddings in America now have a groom cake, according to TheKnot.com.[3]

---

[3] http://editorial.designtaxi.com/news-infgroomguide311014/5.jpg

Groom cake is a separate cake for the groom. It's often a novelty cake and not virginal white. It's often richer, or, rather, it often actually tastes good. It's often in the form of a novelty shape, or theme. Maybe a football helmet or a Tardis or something. This is a tradition that started in England but really took off in the southern US, where it's still a big thing. In the old days, it sat on another table. That still happens, but awe also see them sitting side by side with the wedding cake, and also sometimes even on top of the wedding cake. Hey. I don't know. I'm from Alaska.

If you want to do this, go for it. Might be fun. If not, don't sweat it. Unless you're from the south, in which case it might be worth copping to tradition. If you make a synthesizer or guitar groom cake, please send me a picture.

Snacks

There are two primary times that snacks are useful: during the cocktail hour and late into the night, if your wedding goes late. By and large, what we see here is that most wedding food caterers are happy to include the cocktail hour hors d'oeuvres in their bid for the dinner, and you will use the same servers to put out (on tables) or pass (on trays) the snacks around. You should include "passed apps" in your RFP for your dinner bid, then work out the final selection once you've selected a vendor.

A late night snack is something else entirely. Typically, this will be purchased from some scrumptious pizza or hot dog or taco place you love nearby. It'll show up around 11 or 12, when everyone's drunk, and it'll keep the party rockin' for another few hours. I recently hit up a wedding where the pizzas showed up at the after party and it was amazing. We did a midnight pizza party at our wedding that kept most people on their feet till 4 AM. Also, it was super fun to show up at Vinnie's Pizza the day before with a wad of cash and order 80 pizza pies.

Booze

Let's talk about the booze situation for your reception. Now, before we begin, of *course* – of course – you don't *have* to buy alcohol for your reception. You need not have any alcohol at your wedding at all. Some people do this. It is your day, your party, your right. If you want to take this course of action, more power to you. I advise you to consult the caveat above regarding non-traditional serving approaches, and be sure to let people know what to expect in advance.

Now, with that caveat out of the way, for many people, alcohol and the social slipperiness that it provides is an important component of any good wedding reception. There are a lot of people at your wedding, who may not know each other, or perhaps know each other too much, if you know what I mean, nudge nudge, wink wink. Alcohol can help everyone get along better. As the Radiohead song "Drunken Punch Up at a Wedding" implies, things can also go horribly, horribly awry.

Encouraging Moderation

This fine line should be your guide. You want the alcohol to make things flow like silky smooth R&B, not encourage the party to descend into sheer chaos. Unless you're part of certain punk rock gangs who like that sort of thing, or perhaps a member of the Pogues. Other than that, this advice applies. Concretely, this means that while access to booze should be easy and free (to the extent you can manage it) for your wedding guests, there does need to be some judicious, shall we say, editing. The selection of booze can play a part in this. I could ramble on and on about the emotional pairings of two drunks who have indulged themselves on various types of libations, but I will confine myself here to simply saying that it can play a part. Nothing but whiskey and gin all night? Bad idea.

The atmosphere of the wedding as a whole can play a part as well. People subconsciously know it's poor form to be too argumentative in a festive atmosphere, and have been conditioned specifically against getting too carried away at weddings. Nonetheless some settings are more risky than others. Vegas, paradoxically, seems to be helpful in this regard. You'd think that with all that Sin City surrounding everyone they'd be a bit more stabby, but it doesn't seem to be the case. My suspicion is that the extra oxygen pumped into the air at the casinos keeps us from getting too tanked. Other venues seem to make people a bit more miserable and, thus, cranky when they get drunk. Church basements, hotel convention rooms, and other dreary rooms can exacerbate things.

Pay attention, too, to the accessibility of the booze. This is especially important if you have a few alcoholic friends who have a tendency to go off. Here we insert the usual caveats about the ills of alcoholism, and our duty to help our friends, but today we are speaking of the practical matters of getting your reception to go off without a hitch. If the alcoholics in your social circle aren't belligerent or grabby, then your worry will be less. Hopefully they will just pass out in a corner. Also should you have no alcoholic friends, you lucky duck, then these bits of advice can go unheeded. I should caution, though, that with the olds, we know not their past lives, and the last thing you want is for your Aunt Martha to decide that she can handle gin again, have five glasses, and dredge up the family's past drama in front of your new family and best friends.

Specifically what we are advising here is two things: first, in a high-risk environment, don't have servers constantly refill wine glasses. It's a fun thing at a nice restaurant when someone is keeping your glass constantly full, but at a wedding it will have practical implications. Everyone will drink more, so it may have a financial impact, depending on your arrangement. More relevantly, someone who knows they should control themselves has a harder time saying no in these situations. It's one thing to say "yes, I would like another glass of wine" for all to hear, and for their spouse to notice. It's another when someone is quietly pouring the wine into their glass all night. It makes it harder for them to keep count - often these people know their limits - and eliminates the guilt of quaffing by not having to explicitly ask for more.

Secondly, pay attention to the availability and quantity of bartenders. It's not necessarily a bad thing to have to wait a few moments in a one-or-two-person-deep line for a drink. Too many bars may encourage people to get up and get anther drink more often than necessary. Think upon, as well, the topic of whether you want to keep the full bar open during dinner. One approach is to have the cocktail hour, and then only serve beer and wine through dinner, re-opening the full bar for the reception. It's true that pros know this trick well and spend most of the cocktail hour ferrying multiple drinks to their dinner seat, but it can still have an impact.

Encouraging Excess

All this out of the way now, let us switch gears and talk about best practices for throwing a reception of which Kingsley Amis would approve. One in which decent, right thinking drinkers can get their drink on without obstacle, and without viewing the host couple as being miserly. For a true professional drinker will spot most of the techniques for keeping them from their booze, and while they will perhaps think of this as an effort on your part to keep them from hurting themselves and thus thank you for it, it's far more likely they will simply judge you as a cheap bastard.

We should interject here that there is a difference between being cheap and being poor. Being cheap is no open bar. Being poor is one that may only go for an hour. Being cheap is small pours. Being poor is avoiding the top shelf brands. Being cheap is not providing anything at all for the toast. Being poor is one small glass of prosecco. Being poor is a cash bar at the afterparty. People understand. They don't expect you to blow all of your money on them. It's the 21st century the man is bringing us all down, income inequality is through the roof. People know we're not all made of money. Well, except for a couple of Silicon Valley VCs. They seem to think we are. Whoops. Sorry. Wrong book.

That said, here's some tips for really ripping it up and going all out. And believe me, people will notice.

Full bar at the cocktail hour. Full bar open through dinner. Liberal pours at the bar. During certain types of open bars, this will begin to happen naturally if the bartenders are having a good time, but often you may need to instruct the bar to do so. It's worth a chat if you are using a venue you're not familiar with. Ample bartenders to reduce wait times. As high up as you can go on the shelf towards the top shelf brands. People handing out wine and champagne from trays during the cocktail hour and toasts, reducing the rush to the bar at the beginning of the cocktail hour.

And an open bar as long as you can can afford to fund.

Signature cocktails – some made-up drink in keeping with the theme of your wedding – are a touch 'o class. Consider offering one. Or two. By all means. People love that type of thing. When dreaming them up, do take a moment to think about the rapidity with which the bartenders can make the cocktail and whether you're serving them exclusively, or whether they're just another thing on the menu. The latter is preferable to the professional drinker, who may try one or two signature cocktails early on but would really rather, eventually, get down to drinking their regular poison. Barrel aged cocktails can be very classy, and easy to quickly serve.

Practical Matters Regarding Negotiating Your Booze Contract

Booze is procured in four ways for receptions. Three of them are through the vendors: you can pay by the person, by the hour, or by the drink. Additionally, depending on the venue, the fourth option is to buy your own booze and hire some bartenders to serve it. Leaving aside the fourth option for a moment, let's discuss the other three. The trick here is math. How many drinks does each person drink? The math is a relatively straightforward affair.

So, for example, if the bar charges $1000 an hour, or $20 a person, and your reception is four hours and you have 100 people, with the by the hour option you are paying $2.5 a person per hour for your drinks. With the by-the-person option, you are paying $5 per person per hour. The former is a better bet. To compare these options to the by-the-drink pricing you will need the cost of an average drink at this bar (including, or not including, top shelf, depending on whether you're serving it), and then figure each person will have one drink per hour.

If you are serving top shelf, assume the average drink price will trend higher, towards the top shelf cost. Not everyone will do so, but a good number of guests will get the best booze they can for free. This has killed me in certain party booze contract negotiations in the past. Next, you need to factor in the booziness of your friends in these calculations. If one drink an hour seems absurd, you can tweak your number. However do remember that though you or your close friends may be heavy drinkers, not everyone will be.

Most importantly, and though it may pain you to hear this – remember that people will leave. If your wedding is 200 people and your reception is six hours, by the last hour of the wedding, there may only be 75 people left. If you took a pure "by the hour" approach, and the math worked great in hour one for 200 people, by hour six you're probably paying an exorbitant amount for the remaining 75 people's drinks. There are two simple ways to handle this. First, you can endeavor to negotiate a changeover in the pricing at a certain hour. Say that you're doing a by the hour charge for the first three hours, and a by the person charge for the next three. Not all venues will accommodate this, because, honestly, how is anyone supposed to count the number of people remaining at a reception three hours in. Some venues won't mind - especially if they're making their real money off of the venue rental or the food. Alternatively, if they won't accept this, you can roll the dice and say you'll pay by the drink after X number of hours. I find this to be a pretty good approach. Few people – a very few – ramp UP their drinking after 2-3 hours of drinking. Far more common everyone gets good and liquored up in the first couple hours and then drinks a sustaining amount. Yes, there will be a few rounds of shots amongst the more exuberant types (quite likely your groomsmen), but the price overall should be much lower in those later hours. Take care not to pay full hourly cost as the party size dwindles.

If neither of these approaches are available to you due to a particularly intractable venue, the best thing is to just cut the party shorter and head to the after party, where you can have different payment terms. This could be as simple as a card down at the after party bar or, even better, let the drunk guests pay for themselves.

A final option to be discussed is the time-honored tradition of buying the booze yourself. This is a logistically intense, yet wonderfully affordable approach – especially useful for off-the-beaten-path weddings and receptions, and receptions in private houses. The great thing about booze is it keeps, so you can buy it in advance – if you have a place to store it. But do think through the timing and purchase of the booze, as well as giving it time to get cold (you'll need to plan for ice as well). Work it into your timeline.

Even a budget planner who bought their own booze should consider enlisting a bartender - either from a professional service or from a friend. Be warned: the whole thing can be a pain in the butt to deal with on your wedding day. Delegate. But it can be super cheap, and you may also have some left over which can be quite nice.

Without a bartender, you will soon see what pigs your friends are. Chaos will reign. The beer cups will be used for gin and tonics, spillage will wantonly waste good booze, and many, many guests will get too drunk. Every town has relatively affordable bartender companies, which can add a touch of class to a budget wedding for not too much money. Worst case – get some friends to take shifts, or stick to bottled beer and wine. Some "professional" wedding venues will let you buy your own booze and they will serve it, or let you bring in some third party bartenders.

There exists, on the Internet, several sites that allow you to enter a few variables – how many guests, how many drinks per guest, what kind of booze you're serving, how much it costs in your area — to figure out a booze budget. These are handy when buying your own booze. Work it into your budget at the outset. Often alcohol is a not insubstantial part of the budget. And it's no fun to run out.

Chapter 6: Printed Matter

Getting Started

You are going to get a lot of stuff printed. The invitations are the most notable, but by the time those are printed you'll already have done your save the date cards. We've talked about how you will need a visual theme for your wedding, and the save the date cards are a good place to establish that. Also by this point, having chosen your "look and feel" for your wedding, you should have a graphic designer in place. Now you're going to need to get everything else printed, most notably the invitations.

Printing need not be expensive to be elegant. If you were to pick up any other wedding planning guide, right here would be a whole section on engraving and embossing and foil and thermography. If you've hired a wedding planner, they'll have a preferred printer or two who "specialize in weddings." Avoid all of this. You'd never know it, given how much the world is moving to the Internet, but there is still a robust word of small, independent printers in the United States. Find a hip local printer near you. We found one three blocks from our house. Start

Googling around. There is almost certainly some swarthy hipster not too far from your house using a letterpress or a screen printing kit to make some totally beautiful, hipsteriffic prints. Wedding planning man Mike advises to look for interesting alternatives. "We printed our wedding invitations at a company that prints weekly newspapers. The newspaper added a really interesting aesthetic and were able to be folded out into a big poster."

Alternatively do it all over the internet. Seriously. Don't waste your money on fancy expensive invitations. Unless you're some sort of high society denizen where these things are expected. This is not the time to put on airs. The money is not worth it. Stationary. Envelopes. Oh, god, the amount of money some people expect you to spend on envelopes. It's madness. Stop the madness.

When getting things printed, the importance of proofing cannot be stressed enough. Especially with internet presses. Give yourself plenty of time. Look over everything you submit, and everything you receive back from the printer. Have other people double and triple check it. I worked for some time at a small local printing press, and this was where we made most of our money – correcting errors. It can easily double your cost. I had a friend recently ship out her RSVP cards with a typo. Talk about a pain!

Calligraphy

Regarding the addresses on your invitation envelopes: people get these things calligraphy'ed. They just do. Everyone does. I thought about bucking the system on this, but you know what? It's actually not that hard to find reasonably priced calligraphy services, AND they will also put the stamps on and mail them out, and that service is just so worthwhile, why not get the calligraphy done too. You can find these peeps on Google. The thing here, though, is that you absolutely must have the addresses right. Now, you should have a pretty good address list, because you sent out save the date cards, and anyone whose address was wrong will have had their cards returned to you, and you will have had a chance to fix it. But it's important to get this right. You don't want people to not get their invitations, and you don't want to pay a calligrapher to redo things – it's needlessly expensive and takes time.

Good calligraphers tend to have seasonal backlogs, and if you delay, you're going to pay more, so like all things, do it as early as possible.

Mailing

Mailing invitations is a BITCH. It's tedious and time consuming. You want to use a service for this if you can. Many calligraphers offer this service as an add on to their calligraphy, since they're addressing the envelopes already. I strongly encourage you to use them. Outsource outsource outsource.

If you were smart and you are using pre-made, standard sized envelopes you can send them off to the calligrapher, with the stamps, in advance of even getting the invites printed, then you could supply all of that to the printer and have them mail them out immediately upon printing (and proofing) but that is some next-level order of organization I do not possess, so more power to you if you pull that off.

Do think about your stamps. We found some stamps we liked and mailed them on to the calligrapher with the invitations and envelopes.

Invitations

The invitation is the *piece de resistance* of your wedding printing.

Let's pause for a moment and spare a hand-clap for some restraint and reason. You can get lost in this stuff. You can suddenly think you're a failure in life if you don't spend $80 each on invitations. Don't do it. Seriously. Don't waste the money. The other obstacle I see is that people get sucked into internet viral photos and videos of amazing wedding gimmicks and feel like they have to keep up with the joneses. People go insane for these things, and the pressure to do something unique and memorable can be intense. Personally, I don't think it's worth it. I also can say with confidence that nobody attending your wedding cares. Moreover, do you really want a wedding where everyone thinks back in ten years, "Gee, that invitation was SO CLEVER." No. No one cares.

You'll want the invitation to state your names, the date, the venue and the time at the very least. Traditionally, the invitation was "sent out" by the parent of the bride, or both sets of parents and used full names for everyone and said things like "Mr. and Mrs. Joe X and Mr. and Mrs. John Y invite you to the wedding of..." It was very formal, and a little bit sexist, but kind of fun because you'd go "holy moly Jane's middle name is Excelsior? Who knew?" You may feel free to take this traditional approach if it appeals to you, but honestly in this real world pretty much anything goes. Do what works for you two, and matches the charter of your wedding.

Along with the invitation, it is traditional to mail a few other items. Modern technology is slowly chipping away at the requirement that you include these items, but things are moving slowly.

RSVP Cards

The RSVP Card is a small card that is pre-printed and allows the invitee to let you know whether they're coming to the wedding or not. They also include a small, pre-addressed envelope that is already stamped. The invitee marks down whether they're coming or not and mail it off. Decisions here include the big "digital or analog" choice. On top of that, you may want to include a space for number of guests, though be careful to not imply via the printing that solo guests can bring a +1 if they really can't (if you've given everyone a +1, no worries here). Finally, some people ask about dietary preferences in the RSVP card. Some people even ask about specific menu items, but if you ask me that is some next-level stuff for the hard core.

Permanent Address Cards

In the long-forgotten days of yore, an era known as the 50's which you can learn about from such historical documents as *I Love Lucy*, couples included a card with their new permanent address on it. Because, you know, they were virginal and children, and now they were taking a big step into adulthood. Today in America, well, maybe not so much. I haven't seen one of these in years. But if you're feeling fancy, or are actually two young adults about to make a home together for the first time, well, hey. Go for it.

Maps and Directions

Another tale of woe from eras long forgotten: once upon a time, people had to get around the world without a smart phone in their pocket. They used these historical curiosities called paper maps to help them find their way. People kept bound books of paper maps in their car of their local environs. When inviting people to an event, organizers would assist the attendees by providing a small paper map, including directions on how to get to the event. People don't do this anymore. Put the address on the invitation and be done with it. Maybe, MAYBE, if you have some difficult, off-the-grid hidden spot, you might want to include a few pointers (turn left at the balloons onto the old farm trail), but really, these are edge cases. Few people do this anymore.

Reception Card

If you're hosting a separate reception from the original wedding at a different venue, some people like to include a separate invitation for the reception. This is a less-fancy invitation in the same envelope, which just makes me wonder why the first one needs to be so fancy. If you don't want to deal with this, you can ignore it and simply say "reception to follow." Though if you do this, make sure that a) the reception is in the same place as the ceremony, b) you have provided transportation to and from, so they don't need to know where it is, or c) you put the destination for the reception online at your wedding website. In any case, if the reception is at a different location, at the very least say "Reception at X to follow" so they can GPS the thing. It is, I assure you, entirely acceptable to omit this extra piece of dead tree if you won't want to incur the extra cost.

Envelopes

Regardless of what else you stuff into it with the invitation, you will need envelopes. A good approach is to use pre-made envelopes and matching stock. Don't go for anything custom, it just gets stupidly expensive. Okay let's rephrase that: be aware that you don't *have* to do custom stuff, and have your printer and designer work together so that you can make use of cheaper, pre-made envelopes with matching paper stock. Be explicit on this to both of them.

Thank You Cards

May as well do this now, so they match everything. You're going to have to send them out eventually, so get them printed now, while you're used to blowing money on dumb stuff that won't improve the quality of your life in the future. Don't forget the envelopes, because, oh, the embarrassment of sending thank you cards in non-matching envelopes? *Quelle Horreur.*

Programs

The Wedding Program is a great little thing. It outlines the ceremony, but more usefully it lets everyone attending the wedding know who, say, that cute bridesmaid or that dish of a best man is. Useful stuff. We discuss it in detail elsewhere. It's also nice for your hipster friends to look at your processional and recessional music selection and judge you. You can also add some additional information to the program, especially if your wedding is at the same venue as the reception. For example, we told our guests there would be vegetarian and vegan options for dinner, a late night pizza party, and that it was entirely okay to sneak out of the reception without saying goodbye because who wants to spend their whole wedding night saying goodbye to people? If you're considering using guests as manpower – for example, having them move chairs inside after an outdoors wedding, into an indoor reception area – consider having it printed in the program.

Wedding Programs have become a thing. People obsess over them almost as much as the invitations, and there are a bazillion stupendously creative examples of them on the web. Don't fret too much about keeping up with the joneses. Unless you're the next incarnation of millennial Martha Stewart, make something nice and move on.

Placeholder Cards

If you've chosen to put your guests through the hell that is assigned seating at the reception, then you may as well go ahead and print little placeholder cards. Now, this isn't as easy as it sounds. One would think that it'd simply be a matter of printing a bunch of cards with people's names on them, and setting them at tables, but no no no. People don't do that. You have to independently invent a complex and obscure system by which the various attendees of the wedding are assigned their tables. Maybe make them hit a water balloon with a dart or invent cold fusion. Whatever absurd system you choose to do after subjecting yourself to too many wedding videos, for god's sake make it easy to navigate quickly, so your guests aren't all bunched up in a corner for an hour. People want to find their tables quickly so they can go and stake out a seat that is facing the action, leave their purse there, or place three drinks by their plate so they have enough of a supply for the whole dinner. Be a dear and make this bearable. The ideal situation would include the rapid procurement of a drink. Better yet, do away with the whole god forsaken system and let people have some free will.

Other Stuff

Matchbooks. Fans. People like fans if it's hot in the venue. Banners, trading cards, what have you. People like to leave little gifts for their guests, and some of them may be printed. We made matchbooks. Four thousand of them, because we wanted them in color, and that was the only place I could find that made matchbooks in full color in a reasonable amount of time. You may run into this as well. There are printers and there are wedding printers. Wedding printers effectively make money on this additional stuff because they let you do small print runs, and they mark it up. It was literally cheaper for us to buy 4,000 matchbooks than it was to buy 500. As ever, more time to investigate and research is better. Go off the beaten path, and look at commercial printers that specialize in small businesses. There are a ton of them, it's a competitive market, and much cheaper than wedding printers.

Man Nup

Chapter 7: Decor

Decorating for the Ceremony

Decorating for your wedding is a very different undertaking, depending on whether you're doing the ceremony and the reception in one place or not. It is, obviously, easier to decorate one space than two. If you're using two venues, well, it will be hard for you or your paid planner to be in both places at once before the wedding. It'll be hard enough for you to be in even one place – since you should be with your future spouse, family and bridal party getting ready for the big day. Hopefully one of the two venues you have chosen for your wedding looks good on its own. If this is the case, you can focus primarily on the other venue. Also remember: if you're doing the ceremony in one spot, and the reception in another, you're going to be spending a larger part of the day and evening in the latter venue.

Let's start with decorating for the ceremony.

If you're decorating a venue that is just being used for the ceremony, well, you're in for a ride. People get very, very neurotic about decorating for the ceremony. And yet, much of it seems pointless.

Presumably wherever you chose for your ceremony, you chose because the place because, you know, it's actually kind of nice. Run with that. Just run with that.

Someone, somewhere down the line, is going to put an impressive amount of effort into convincing you that this relatively gorgeous physical space can only be made bearable by investing large amounts of cash on things like flowers, ribbons, bows, and, god help us all, aisle runners. Okay, I suppose there may be some traditional purpose for these, and maybe you have just dreamed about these things since you were a child (honestly, what is wrong you?). And you know what? Aisle runners are actually not even that expensive. You can get a cheap one for like ten bucks. But it looks cheap. And a good one is at least 10 times more. So suddenly you are spending a hundred bucks on a piece of paper that you are going to put on the floor, march over twice, and throw away. If this is appealing to you, feel free to mail me a hundred dollars. I will step on it and then keep it from you.

You don't need big bows on your pews with comely ribbons draped between them. You don't need candles (well, unless you're a goth, that would be kind of sweet — like the Wrapped Around Your Finger video by the Police). Book a nice venue and bob's your uncle.

But if that's not enough for you? Well, let's dig a little deeper.

Flowers

Flowers are, admittedly, the one thing that do tend to spruce up an already nice venue. They are very pretty. They smell nice. And, really, what's a wedding without flowers.

Well, a cheaper one, for a start. Flowers are insanely expensive. Stupidly, insanely expensive. I mean, they grow in the ground. They literally come from the earth. It's strange that they should be so expensive. Honestly, the best thing to do is to not get any flowers. If you can get away with this, you should do it.

The odds are, however, that you will not be able to get away with this. After all, the bride is almost certainly gonna need a bouquet. And that's just the beginning. Yes, bouquets can be hand made, and inexpensive, and crafty, but that's not really your call. You have to default towards flowers, or turn the project over to your spouse. The thing about flowers is there's no upper limit. Your two other biggest expenses in this shindig are going to be food and the venue, but both of those can only get so expensive, once you choose your vendors. I mean, we can only eat so much. But flowers? If you try hard, you can put flowers on anything. ANYTHING. Flowers on dresses and flowers on suits. Flowers in our hands and flowers in our hair. Flowers on the pews and flowers at the door and flowers on the altar or stage and flowers at the reception. Flowers in the restroom and even by the closet. Flowers everywhere. You can literally just keep buying more flowers, and someone will encourage you to do so. I suspect someone, somewhere, has had a wedding that took place entirely within flowers. I actually went to a wedding at a flower shop once. Not kidding.

Broadly speaking, flowers fall into three categories: wedding party flowers, ceremony flowers and reception flowers. The wedding party flowers are the most important, and few people skimp on these completely. Next on the scale are flowers for the ceremony venue, adding some class. Personally, I think reception flowers are a waste of money, but you might be into them. They are, however, definitely the easiest to cut out if you're on a budget.

Let's talk about the wedding party flowers. Working down from the bride's bouquet we have the bridesmaid's bouquets, which are smaller versions of the bridal bouquet. Then we have boutonnieres for the groom, groomsmen, family, and ushers. Do a full count. Order one or two extra. They break easily. Beyond that? It's really your call. Don't forget the kids – if you have a kiddy ringbearer or flower petal tosser,

consider them getting some junior corsages and boutonnieres.

Turning to the ceremony venue, the florist
will try and get to you to drape the entire venue in
flowers. Some flowers are nice, but they may not be
necessary, especially if you've chosen a picturesque
venue that looks splendiferous on its own. Flowers
for the entry way, flowers for the altar. The pews. It
can add up. My friend Mike concurs, and advises to
"try and find a venue that doesn't need a lot of outside stuff to look beautiful. When you do that flowers and balloons and arches and all of that junk isn't
necessary."

The tricky thing about flowers is that if you
want to have a "normal" wedding, the flower aesthetic
really flows from the bride and her dress. So this isn't
a thing you're going to be able to do on your own.
You're going to have to consult with your bride on a
few of the particulars with the flowers. In my case,
Emma said, "I want white roses, bundled tight, and
you can deal with the rest." Bless her soul. Easy as pie.
I whipped up a quick Pinterest board of some bridal
bouquets with white roses, tightly bundled, and had
her do a quick "yes, yes, no." That was enough for me
to run with and handle the rest with the florist. Most
brides care about their flowers and their bridesmaid's
flowers. How much they care about the rest can be

variable. Consult the appropriate amount.

There are florists and there are florists and there are florists. There's the kind of shop you can just walk into and get some flowers. There are the full service shops that do deliveries and everything else. And there are the specialists who only handle weddings and special events. The latter type is the best, and if you can afford it you should go for a specialist. If you're on a budget, use a reputable full service shop and confine yourself to the bouquets and boutonnieres.

Like most wedding vendors, I find communicating by email initially is a good bet, as it indicates you're working with a vendor who is comfortable with using email so you won't have to go in for a million meetings. You'd think in the 21st century everyone would be used to email *at a minimum* for a communications took, let alone Facebook Messenger, Slack, what have you. *But no.* As ever, florists will want to get you in a series of endless appointments, instilling confusion and doubt, and encouraging you to spend a little extra money to be safe. Avoid as many of these as possible. Send over your Pinterest board, get estimates by email, and do the bulk of your communications by email. Cut back any unnecessary expenses. Be vigilant. If you do everything right, you can get by with only meeting your florists once. Really, once they realize you're comfortable with doing everything over the internet, they are pretty content to do it too. Less work for them. My florist was content to send over photos in emails, and I approved everything over email as well.

The biggest risk with the florists is that they might not show up on time the day of the event. I don't know why, but this seems to happen more often than people think. I have a theory here: I think it's because of the multiple types of florists, and people having some confusion about what they're actually buying. It's far less likely that a professional wedding florist is late – they know the drill – than, say, if you bought your flowers from a florist in the mall (oh my god I used to have the biggest crush on the florist in the mall in Boston) and just ask for a delivery on Sunday to such-and-such a place. Factor this into your vendor decision-making. Make it clear at what time they are supposed to be at the venue (also sending them a full copy of your wedding itinerary), and make it clear when the ceremony is. If you're going budget, and you're getting your flowers from a full service shop or a walk-in shop, make sure you have someone to transport the flowers in a timely manner, and make sure they will have everything you need in stock.

Many brides have a thing for saving the bouquet. It's this whole thing. People can be strange. You can do it yourself by hanging it upside down, or you can send it off to get some crazy girly art made out of it. But I mean, why would you do such a thing? However, consult your bride on their desires. She might be really into it. Maybe she's going to hang it upside down, dry it, and put it into a custom bridal bouquet box, which is a thing you didn't know existed until now. You know, hypothetically.

Oh, and don't forget the petals for your flower boy/girl/person. And make sure the florist doesn't either.

Traditional Flourishes

Throwing rice or confetti or blowing bubbles are time-honored traditional wedding practices, symbolizing fertility, abundance and wealth or something along those lines. You should at least consider whether they have a place in your ceremony. Rice has been on the way out for some time – there's a myth about it involving birds not being able to digest it, but that's mostly bunk. Really. It's even been empirically tested.[4] Nonetheless, the myth remains, as do laws banning the practice in some jurisdictions. Many wedding professionals find this to be just fine. In reality rice is messy, it's hard to walk on, it hurts when it hits you in the face, it gets into your clothes

---

[4] "Against the Grain." Snopes.com, no date. http://www.snopes.com/critters/crusader/birdrice.asp

and it's a pain to clean up. Some of this is true of confetti as well, so we see most confetti use inside. Bubbles are a good time, harder to clean up inside, less difficult outside. Note: in Morocco they throw raisins and figs.[5] Why not? Delicious wedding rain.

Let's not forget the cans on the back of the car – another time-honored wedding cliche falling by the wayside. Where on earth did this silly tradition come from? Google will proffer a lot of theories: warding off evil spirits[6], a Tudor custom involving throwing shoes at the departing wedding couple, which was either done in a garter-like tradition where whomever hit the carriage got lucky[7], or perhaps the leather in shoes warded off evil sprits, neatly tying those two theories together.[8] In Ancient Egypt, supposedly, the father of the bride gave the groom his daughter's

---

[5] Alexandra Ochoa. "The Tradition of Throwing Rice at a Wedding." Que Rica Vida. 27 November 2012. http://www.quericavida.com/whats-rico/traditions-and-family/the-tradition-of-throwing-rice-at-a-wedding

[6] "Wedding Traditions – tying tin cans to the back of the wedding car." Handmade Weddings, 16 July 2013, http://www.handmadeweddings.co.uk/wedding-traditions-tying-tin-cans-to-the-back-of-the-wedding-car/

[7] "3 Bizarre Wedding Customs Nobody Questioned (Until Now!)." Mental Floss, no date. http://mentalfloss.com/article/17737/3-bizarre-wedding-customs-nobody-questioned-until-now

[8] "Why do they tie cans to the back of a car for a wedding?." Yahoo.com, no date. https://answers.yahoo.com/question/index?qid=20100630050931AAMudbt

sandal, finalizing the transaction. The research dynamos at Bed Bath Beyond helpfully elaborate that "[s]ince shoes were considered a phallic symbol, it was also thought to promote fertility for the newlyweds and later shoes were tied to the getaway car."[9] They should know, right? My favorite explanation comes from the wedding sages at Esurance, who claim that the practice "stems from the old French tradition of charivari, in which friends (and frenemies) would show up late at night outside the home of the just-married couple and serenade them noisily with pots, pans, and anything else that made a racket. This would continue until the newlyweds invited the revelers in for refreshments. French settlers brought the practice to the American frontier, where it was known as shivaree[10]." This has the added benefit of being so specific as to seem like it was actually properly researched, unlike this paragraph, so, hey, let's go with that.

None of these tidbits of information that I found on the web, were sourced – the authors just stated them, and didn't provide source material citations. It's quite possible all of this is bunk. And I am guilty of propagating bunk. But we add these quasi-factual talking points not for edification, so much

[9] "Just For Fun." Bed Bath and Beyond. No date. http://www.bedbathandbeyond.com/store/guide/just-for-fun/bg10236

[10] Ellen Hall. "4 Weird Car Traditions Explained." Esurance.com, 2 July 2013, http://blog.esurance.com/4-weird-car-traditions-explained/#.VkOq99-rTOY

as to equip you: they'll come in handy in the endless amounts of wedding banter you'll have to endure for the next several months. Think of them not as truths (because who the hell knows) but as arrows in your quiver of shooting the breeze about weddings.

Honestly, I haven't seen the cans on the back of a car in... ten years? Twenty? It might be kind of terrific if you wanted to try that, but be considerate of your neighbors?

These sorts of things can add a nice touch if you take the time to do them thoughtfully and right. You'll need to plan ahead for them. Get the bubbles into the hands of guests in advance (remembering our advice about how leaving gift bags at the hotel only covers some guests). Arrange with your groomsmen or ushers to tie the cans onto the car – also checking local regulations and planning with the car rental agency to make sure it's allowed. By now you know my love of rental companies, so if you can find one that rents confetti cannons and you go that route (indoors, to allow for safe cleanup), you have my genuine admiration. Tweet me a picture of it. I would love to see that.

Ring Pillows

One thing I'm sorta into if you have a ring bearer is a ring pillow. I mean, come on. It's a little pillow for rings. And you don't even use the real rings on the pillow! Dada.

Again, unverified sources claim this practice came from Ancient Egypt (man, they really had weddings figured out there) where it was customary to bring in jewels on ornamental pillows.[11] Others claim it was from medieval times, where the ring was brought in on a sword. So presumably they eventually replaced the sword with the least sword-like thing they could find? No idea. Seriously, all of these people are just making these histories up. Don't trust the internet for anything.

It's a nice little useless piece of absurdity, which can be yours for like $10 on Amazon, cute little fake rings included. What do you do with this thing after your wedding? I have no idea. But, come on. A pillow! For rings. Why not. Plus it'll make everyone think you really did think of anything. They'll secretly be impressed with your planning prowess. Nice little bonus on your wedding day.

Decorating for the Reception

When decorating for your reception, many of the same principles apply as decorating for your ceremony. Many of the things people will want you to buy are frippery and unnecessarily expensive. A nicer ven-

[11] "Wedding Traditions: The History of the Wedding Ring Bearer," Saphire Event Group, 26 April 2012, http://www.saphireeventgroup.com/blog/wedding-traditions-what-is-the-history-of-the-wedding-ring-beare/

ue is less expensive to make look good than an ugly venue. Hand-made decorations are a nice touch but very labor intensive and a potential strain on friendships. And never forget: you can get anything from rental companies. Theater and lighting rental companies are especially useful here. We needed a very large draping curtain for our wedding, along with some giant star-shaped lanterns. A lighting rental company found both, and brought the staff to set them up and string the lights over a cavernous room 40 feet high. I was all too happy to pay someone to handle all of that.

If you're going for a rather small reception, in a very fancy place, you may consider extending your flower purchase to some nice flowers at the reception venue. Doubly so if you're using one venue for both ceremony and reception. I find that flowers at receptions, however, are usually an unnecessary expense. If the place is gorgeous, you won't really notice the flowers, and if it's not, they're only going to help so much, and people will be preoccupied with fun anyhow. Also, as we've noted, flowers are hella expensive. Reception flowers are best confined to weddings in a single venue.

Wedding planning man Richard tells us of what he learned working in the floral industry, and more affordable ways to make a room look great.

Man Nup

"When I started working in NYC I designed and built websites for high end floral event companies and one of the best things I was ever taught was that filling a space with flowers was the least cost effective way of designing, and that filling a room up with lighting was the best. When I had the opportunity to plan my own wedding I was able to test this theory out in real life. Lindsay and I were married in an old factory with beautiful industrial brick walls that were about 40 feet high. I worked a deal out with the DJ to provide uplighting around the entire base of the venue for only $700 and the place looked fantastic. Our entire floral budget for our 150 person wedding was slightly less than $2,000, had we tried to fill the room up with flowers it would have been many several times more than that."

The atmosphere of your reception is far more festive than the ceremony itself. This lends the ability to bring in additional types of decorations. Specifically, I am thinking of bad-ass lights, disco balls and smoke machines. Who doesn't love a disco ball? Remember that setting these things up can be a bitch, and it's easiest to have paid experts from the rental company or venue handle these tasks. Though be warned: just the other day I was talking to a guy who told me a story about how a giant disco ball fell from the ceiling of Radio City Music Hall and almost killed one of my favorite musicians.

(My friend Doug notes: "I've been in two bars where mirrors fell off the wall onto the heads of patrons. No one was injured, but the bartender was obligated to buy a round. You don't need this on your conscience – no one does.") So, maybe don't get a 10 foot wide one. Also, in terms of smoke machines, in some cities there are some licensing and fire requirements around them. In New York, for example, we had to have a fire marshall on staff to use the smoke machine. This was an extra fee. WHICH I PAID, and forgot to turn on the smoke machine, to my eternal regret. Don't make these kind of major mistakes. Life changing. Seriously.

Take Down

Think a bit about post-ceremony take-down. Obviously most of the rental companies will take down their own stuff and bring it home, but you may be responsible for taking down your own decorations, or the venue may charge a fee. Be sure to discuss this in your rental discussions – and also whether the rental companies can leave stuff over night and pick it up in the morning. This is important for late-going receptions, where it may be exorbitantly expensive to keep the lighting rental personnel around till 4 AM. Some venues are cool with this, others less so. This is the kind of task a wedding planner would handle, but if you are on your own, well, you are on your own.

Man Nup

Chapter 8: AV Club

Tech Nerds

I'm probably showing my age here, but in my days, AV Club in my high school was the audio visual club. It was a group of tech geeks who provided services setting up slide & film projectors, PA systems, and the like for school plays, assemblies, and what have you. It was the redoubt of the enthusiastic nerds who also wanted to be part of creating things like plays and performances. It's since morphed into sort of an IT services department at the larger modern high schools, primarily concerned with tech support for the computers. From what I hear.

Here we will talk about the sound, the photography, the videography, the music, and the tech.

Despite what you may think at first blush, the AV equipment and setup at your wedding will be important. People will need to hear the band, the DJ, the officiant and, most importantly, your vows. You will want photographs, perhaps even a video. Fine-tuning your AV Club can involve a lot of logistical coordination, but it's these details that can make a wedding operate smoothly. Let's face it: even if every single microphone, camera, speaker and turntable breaks down, a wedding can still be marvelous. But they do add that little extra something. Some of it might be vital to you – the music, the photographs. And as in all things wedding related, the sooner you plan it, the more money you can save.

Mic'ing the Ceremony

Putting a microphone into a wedding ceremony is a dicey proposition: it can interfere with the intimacy of the event, it can break down, it can make people uncomfortable. By the same token, it's even more of a bummer to have the world's greatest vows and have no one hear them.

The important thing is research. See if you can attend another event at your venue. Barring that, speak softly from where the wedding will wake place, and see if someone in the back of the venue can hear you. Remember, this is the best-case scenario: it will get even more difficult to hear once the room is filled with human beings who, weirdly, always seem to make noise just being alive. It's strange. Except ninjas. They're silent. Furthermore, let's be aware of the elderly and the hard of hearing, who have trouble hearing even in the best of situations (though there really have been remarkable advances in hearing aid technology these last few years. But I digress). Ask

the venue management if they recommend micro-
phones at the wedding. If so, ask what type they recommend, or if they can provide one.

If you need to wire the place for sound yourself, a cheap PA system and a single microphone on
a stand, placed between you, your betrothed and the
officiant should do the trick. If you are feeling com-
pletist, perhaps one more off to the side for readings.
A small powered speaker or two, raised on stands,
and a small mixing console will do the trick. If AV
club isn't your thing, and the venue is non-existent
or unhelpful, ask a friend who looks like they used to
be in AV club. As a former AV club member I can say
that we enjoy it. Honest. Finally, most professional
musicians – if you've gone that route – can handle
their own PA, but make sure you ask.

The Music

Now let us turn to the most important part
of any wedding ceremony: the music. Okay, maybe
this isn't the most important part for you. And in
fact, I find that the people for whom music is not
that important in life often have a more difficult time
with this aspect of a wedding than those who live and
breathe music. I'll offer a few stylistic bits of advice
for those who feel less able to curate, but these are
mere suggestions. Feel free to ignore them.

Man Nup

There are five aspects of a wedding and a reception for which you need to think of music: prior to the ceremony, the procession/recession, the cocktail hour, the first dance, and the dancing at the reception. We'll talk about each period that music should be thought through at a wedding, and then we'll talk about different means of producing it – live, pre-recorded, or a DJ.

Prior to the Ceremony

This is the music that you are playing when guests are mulling about and getting ready to sit down for the ceremony. This is usually mellow, pretty, classical or classical-sounding music. Instrumental is best, though some etherial female vocals such as the Cocteau Twins wouldn't be totally inappropriate. There are several good string quartets on Spotify, including some that play "the hits," in instrumental form, which might be fun. Bach, Mozart. The giants. These are also good choices. If you have a favorite mellow musical act, feel free to play that. We went with a selection of alternative hits played by a quartet called the Vitamin String Quartet.

Some weddings forgo this altogether. Some go the full-blown string quartet style. Some might have a friend noodling away on an acoustic guitar in the corner. I do believe having something here is better than nothing, and adds a touch of class. It need not be expensive. A DJ would be weird and excessive, unless you're having some sort of electronica wedding, in which case that might be kind of groovy. Google rules apply (yes, there are whole, amazing and robust, websites just for booking string quartets out there. It's kind of amazing).We simply played a bunch of classical music through an iPod at the wedding venue. If this is the approach you're taking, be sure to coordinate with the venue in advance.

We should say a quick word about rights organizations. Long story short, there are these organizations that hold the power in their hand to keep certain venues from playing certain music. I know, it's weird. It's almost certainly not going to be an issue for you – most venues have just paid the flat fee, or are so obscure no one cares. A representative from BMI or ASCAP is not going to burst into your wedding and stop the show. I only bring it up for one edge case: if you are booking your wedding at a heavily legal, unionized, by-the-book venue such as an Opera House in a major city, you'll want to make sure there are going to be no problems. Best way to do this is to just ask the representative from the venue, in an innocent, guileless manner, "So I can play any music I want, right? And bring in my own DJ?" If it's not a problem, they'll look at you like you're weird and go,

"Yeah, of course." But if it is, this is where they'll go all union on you and say, "Oh no, no, *no*. The music has to come from the BMI librar..." Oh god just stop. Better to know in advance.

The Ceremony

This is where the rubber meets the road. These are the songs that you play when the wedding party are walking down the aisle, and then the music for everyone recessing and leaving the ceremony. There are two broad popular approaches here: to play the traditional wedding songs, or to play music that means something to the couple. I gotta say, we've moved so far from the popular wedding marches, that these days I get a real kick out of hearing *Here Comes the Bride* (officially The Bridal Chorus from Richard Wagner's *Lohengrin*), or Mendelssohn's *Wedding March*. It's kind of fantastic. Especially the latter. The other approach is to pick some songs that mean something to you. It adds a personal touch. You can make a note of it in the program. Stylistically, people are all over the place with song selections, and broadly, I say more power to them. I do think a little bit of class is a good thing for the bridal procession, especially. More fun can be had with the procession of the rest of the wedding party (often a separate song), and the recession. But to each his own. We went with a custom instrumentation of Annie Lennox's *Love Song For a Vampire*, made by our friend Sean Drinkwater, and the Vitamin String Quartet's version of the Deep Space 9 theme (yes, we are nerds) for our procession, and a medley of two Mercury Rev songs (*The Dark is Rising* and Opus 40) for our recession. One wedding I went to a few years back had the bride process in to Guns N Roses' *November Rain*, and that ruled.

One logistical note here: pick someone to handle this music and have them practice. You want to get this right. Whether you book a live act or have a friend do it with a Zune (yes!) or something, make sure they are at the rehearsal. The timing of the processionals and recessional is stupidly important and should be rehearsed. You want the recessional music to kick in right after the kiss, when everyone's clapping, to get that magical, romantic moment you dreamed about when you were a wee Disney Prince. It's really awkward if everyone stops clapping, and you're just standing there waiting for your DJ friend to hit play. Practice practice practice.

The Cocktail Hour

The cocktail hour is kind of a great time for music because, if you're playing pre-recorded music, it's the one time you can really step up and own it and play anything you want. I recommend this heartily. Work with your partner to make a playlist of all your favorite songs. Think about how potentially killer this is for a moment. You just got married, you've shared an intimate, private moment with your new spouse and now you're going to go face all of your friends and have a nice drink for a while. And, oh! How nice. EVERY SINGLE SONG YOU LOVE is playing in the background. It really does add to the experience, I promise.

If you've hired a DJ, you can just have them play this playlist for the cocktail hour and really worry about DJing the reception. This is great, especially, if you're at two separate venues – the DJ can be setting up at the reception venue while you simply play an iPod at the first venue. Do make sure that the venue has a PA system. If the venue is separate from the reception venue, and they don't have a PA system, you'll have to figure something out, which can add an extra expense and hassle. But, you know, the music really only needs to be low in the background so no need to go all out on a big PA unless it's a big wedding.

The First Dance

The one song that the two of you may well discuss and obsess over for months in advance of the wedding. You only got one shot. It should be something special to the two of you. But it doesn't have to be the first song you ever heard together or some amazingly overly emotional thing. It can just be a song you both enjoy. Also, I strongly suggest to pay attention to the duration of the song. It's sort of like Karaoke. At one moment you're thinking to yourself "oh I love that song let's karaoke it" and then suddenly you're drunk and you're thinking "Jesus H *Shake Your Love* is like a million years long. How many times can Debbie Gibson say those three words?" The answer is fifty-two, including one time in what can only be called a rap. The two of you will be up there, all alone, trying to look gooey and romantic and sophisticated for the entire duration and that can go on a really long time. Consider this a warning. I've seen one or two, very rare, very special, weddings where the first dance was done by a live quartet or rock band, but this is mostly a pre-recorded affair as I hear it's very hard to get John Lennon to come to your wedding and sing *In My Life*.

Some couples like to go all out and pick some brilliant song and choreograph an entire routine to it. I think this is just great. I've seen a few of these that are amazing, but you know what? It's a lot of work. If it means a lot to you or your partner then why the hell not. Another thing I've seen people do is actually go and take dance lessons. This, to me, seems a bit extreme. I've been to hundreds of weddings, witnessed hundreds of first dances, and not once have I ever heard someone say "Lordy. Those two can NOT dance." *But I will say* I was *just* at a wedding where the groom and his father not only took dancing lessons, but posted the certificate, and danced just the most adorable father-bride dance I have ever seen. Not a dry eye in the house. Also, if you're planning on having children immediately upon getting married, I'll warrant that going to ballroom dancing classes together is good preparation for going to lamaze classes together so, hey. Team building.

The Reception

The reception, the big party, the dancing. Live band or DJ are the popular choices here but I've been to a few where the groom or his new spouse is manning an iPod and things are *off the hook.* Just have fun. You know your friends, you know what kind of music they like. You can go for the traditional wedding songs approach, or something more stylistic.

I do encourage you, however, to think of the older people at your wedding. You know, many older people don't go out much, and don't get many chances to go dancing with their partner. And though I'm only in my 40's and recently married, I can very much see a day on the horizon where going to a wedding is going to be a big night out for me, a special occasion where my wife and I get all dressed up and get to dance. I would like to hear something I know and love, and not just the biological robot rock of the 2040's. Yes, it's fascinating that these musicians in 2040 were grown in a vat, but people like to dance to songs they know, and the older folks aren't going to care that the lead guitarist's dad was a drone. Hopefully before too long *Just Like Heaven* by the Cure will be a classic rock hit. Every year the oldies seem to get a little newer. We're well past Kool and the Gang and Sly and the Family Stone and I think we're almost into Duran Duran and soon we'll be into Stone Roses land. Man, weddings are going to be slammin' in my 60's.

People that love going out dancing every night sometimes overlook this, especially if they met their spouse out dancing. They want to recreate the dancing that they and all their friends love. I went to a wedding recently that did that and it was AMAZING. It was just like being back in that dance club in the 90's. I loved it. But the DJ had the good sense to mix in some oldies. So everyone had a good time. Just this summer I DJ'd a wedding in Alaska, outdoors. The DJ booth was on a dock, and I DJ'd under the midnight sun till 2 AM. At one point the groom hooked up two mics for his two adorable daughters in

their weird pink tutu dresses who were the ring bearer and flower girl. We mixed them in with the music,
quietly, with lots of reverb, and they sang along to
Rihanna and Kraftwerk. I don't know why I'm telling
you this, but, man, it was gorgeous. Singing kids.

Finally, just as I've got a new respect for Mendelssohn's Wedding March, I do kind of love weddings that play the best, most perfectly cliche'd wedding music, from bad current pop and hip hop to the
Electric Slide to Twist and Shout. It can be super fun.
Do whatever you think is best. Don't worry about it
being too "cool." Make sure everyone can have a good
time.

Booking the Music

For each stage of your wedding, the choices for
music are DJs, pre-recorded music or live performers. Many weddings use multiple options for different
parts of the wedding. If you have musician friends or
DJs, you may feel free to ask them for their services.
Playing one song during the procession/recession or
– MAYBE – the pre-ceremony music can be asked of
a friend without thinking too much about paying. If
you're asking your friends to play in a live band or DJ
all night, you should offer to pay for their services.
We mixed it up in our wedding – three friends' bands
and three friends DJing – so no one had to do it for

too long. As ever, be wary of asking your friends to work all night for free.

There are some amazing websites out there for booking wedding bands, from string quartets to rock bands and DJs that specialize in all different sorts of hits. Many specialized wedding venues (especially in Vegas) also have relationships with – or lists of – bands that specialize in weddings. Be warned, wedding bands are not cheap. It's a lucrative business. DJs are cheaper, but they, too, can be expensive. If you're booking someone you've not worked with, or heard at another wedding, or that is recommended by a friend, take time to sit with them and give them a good idea of your tastes. Try to find someone whose tastes align with yours. Most bands and DJs have YouTube or Soundcloud pages now, where you can sample their wares. Be especially careful in booking a club DJ who doesn't do weddings, and might not be as aware of the older people's tastes.

On Smartphones and Laptops

If you're going the pre-recorded route, be sure to make sure everything is actually ON the computer or the iPod. Do NOT rely on streaming. (Clouds bring rain, amirite? Bah dum bump. Thank you. I'll be here all night.) Streaming can be faulty, you might not have good cell reception or good wi-fi. You don't want any hiccups. Some streaming apps offer an "offline sync" capability where the service, such as Spotify, will work even if they have no signal. Take time to learn this. Or make sure the music is directly downloaded onto the device. Test in advance, with the wi fi turned off and the device in airplane mode to make sure everything works.

Photography and Videography

You're going to want a ton of photos taken of your wedding. Maybe even a video. Sometimes I ask myself why. A year in, and I've not looked at my wedding photos much since the week after the wedding. Was all that money worth it? And those photographers. Lurking around, ruining the symmetry and beauty of every scene with their clicking and their snapping and their... just BEING there clogging up the view. There are definitely drawbacks, make no bones about it.

I find that the single best reason for getting wedding photos and videos is for the family. First off, it's an easy way to get a nice gift for everyone in the family the next coming holiday. And honestly, after planning a whole wedding, it's nice to not have to stress about gifts to your new, extended family the next holiday season. I also suspect when I'm 90 years old I will be vaguely wistful and nostalgic looking over those old albums of photos. In any case, if you're completely against having a wedding photographer, feel free and avoid it. But remember, it's one of those decisions that is bigger than you, or even you and your better half. Family members, other people at the wedding, people who couldn't make it – everyone has an opinion and a desire to see the photos.

Booking the Photographer

Let's talk booking a wedding photographer. Usual rules apply: it's better to have a pro than a friend do it (though I find a couple friends as backup, sliding them a couple bucks, can augment a professional photographer in lovely ways). It's better to find your photographer through friend recommendations or your planner's recommendations than from a cold booking. With photographers, things are slightly less risky, since you can actually see their work on other weddings beforehand. And, as with everything, book early. The really good ones book up well in advance – maybe even a year or more. And at the risk of sounding like every other wedding planning sage out there, you really do want your photos to be great, they'll be with you the rest of your life. God, it's cheesy, but it's true.

When talking to prospective photographers, ask them if they handle videography as well – a bundled purchase. Most photographers can provide this service as an add on, or hook you up with the videographer as well, though you may not want to go that route. Even with video becoming more popular, I believe the best bet is still to book the photographer first, and deal with the videographer once you've made your decision.

My friend Mike, who's a web designer in New York, had great luck finding his photographer on Instagram.

"Reach out to photographers you really like... maybe ones on Instagram. We hired this guy from Chicago I followed on Instagram and loved. He flew in and shot the wedding for cheap and did an amazing job."

The first thing you'll notice when you book your wedding photographer and videographer is how many weird, pointless questions they ask. It can be really tedious. In a way, this makes sense. They don't know your friends, they don't know your family politics, and they need to rapidly learn it. They'll ask about the wedding party, the schedule, the various combinations of shots you want. They will ask if there are other events or people at the wedding that are important, and for a little background color on these topics. Answer these as thoughtfully and thoroughly as you can, it really will make a difference. And if you've been ON THE BALL with your wedding planning, the timeline and bridal party questions should be as easy as sharing a Google spreadsheet with the photographer.

Many photographers have package deals. These will be a bundle of products and services such as shooting the ceremony, x hours of the reception, the preparation, and portraits of the wedding party, along with an album or two, or digital access. This may also include your wedding video. I find the best bet here is to get the full resolution digital files of the entire shoot, and do the selections and editing yourself, and buy albums for friends and family online. But this is definitely a more labor intensive approach, and often more expensive. Then again, you know your family and friends better, and thus you know which selections people will like. If you're booking early, you'll have time to compare your photographer's rate for photo albums with that of Flickr, iPhoto, Shutterfly and other services. Ask questions about rights and usage and full resolution files before you book with any wedding photographer. You'll want to work up a list of questions around these topics and send then a request for proposal.

We should say that wedding photographers

and videographers can be stupidly expensive. I do believe that the friend approach is often more feasible with wedding photographers than with, say, caterers or DJs. Many friends are going to want to shoot the wedding anyway, they will know better what is best to shoot, and they will be happy to make a few bucks off of the wedding. If they are already a professional, however, they may not want to take this on. They might just want to enjoy themselves.

If your wedding goes late, you'll also want to make sure the photographer is aware the reception may go past 10 or 11 PM. We forgot to do this and our professional photographer left three hours before the reception ended. Luckily, we compensated with a friend augmenting their services.

The final word goes to Richard, who *insists* you will want to splurge for the video: "Get video. You have to get video even if your lovely future wife tells you not to. There is no replacement to seeing people dance and converse together than through video."

The Wedding Portraits

In addition to shooting the ceremony and the reception, you will want to get a series of wedding portraits taken. This can be a really tedious thing to do on the day of your wedding, but the benefits are huge. You will now have great portraits not only of you and your new spouse, but of your family and their family, your best friends and all of these in every possible combination. Haven't had a nice portrait taken with your mother since you were a kid? Now's the time. All your best mates in one place? Get a classy photo. Think through all the combinations you want, and add a couple extras for spur of the moment ideas. Some photographers charge by the set up in the wedding portraits, but try and shoot (pun intended) for someone who doesn't do this or charges by the hour. An hour should be enough time if you're not too neurotic.

Also think about WHEN in the course of the day you shoot your wedding portraits. Many people do this after the ceremony, before the reception. As a guest, I HATE this. I also would have hated it as a groom. We did ours in the (better) daytime light before our ceremony. It made the rest of the day flow much better, and we didn't have to have the 15 or so most important people at the wedding disappear for an hour right after the big moment.

Photobooths

A photo booth can be quite nice. All the various combinations of your friends go into this booth and get wacky photos taken of them. They get a copy, you get a copy, and everyone get a good laugh. You might get a good make-out photo, maybe even a boob or two. Hey who knows. This is why some of our ancestors came to America, to possibly end up with some black and white photo strips of a blurry boob. And we shouldn't denigrate that sacred contract. Plus, people love photos of themselves. It'll be a hit.

More practically, a photo booth is nice because it is usually relatively cheaper than a photographer (though this is not an absolute) and you get great coverage of the guests at your wedding that the paid photographers may give short shrift to. I also like this because after your wedding you can go through and look at all the photo booth hijinks and see some of the friends with whom you may not have gotten to spend enough. Sad, but true.

There are a few different ways you can pull a photo booth off. You can pay someone to run a "booth," but really just stand there and take photo portraits all night. This is usually pretty straightforward, and doesn't involve any actual physical booth. You just hire a second photographer for this. Some photographers will also do this as an add on. In this situation you need to decorate an area for the photos, and maybe provide some wacky props. People love wacky props.

You can rent an all-in-one photo booth from

one of the many photo booth startups out there. These can be found through your usual internet research routes. I won't name names because it seems like there are literally hundreds of these companies. Many of them will print the photos on the spot, and then make them available online afterwards. The printing of the photos on the spot is a nice touch, so that your guests can, a) see them without hounding the photographer (people love immediate photo feedback) and b) keep a print as a keepsake.

In either instance, you want to make sure your photo booth is easy to find, and people know about it. It's sad when you spend a lot of money on the photo booth and no one uses it because it was in some out-of-the way location and they didn't know about it. The great thing is that once people know about photo booths, they invariably flock to them. So make it somewhere obvious, perhaps put a big sign over it, and even consider printing a message about it on the wedding program. Also, sticking it by a bar or the food works well.

Social Media

In this day and age, everyone's got a camera in their pocket and loves to take and share photos. You can make good leverage of this for your wedding. This allows for the taking of virtually hundreds of additional photos, and in more interesting combinations than your wedding photographer will ever get. Collecting and displaying them all can be a challenge, and in this always-wired hell-age we seem to find ourselves in, the most popular approach seems to be a hashtag for your wedding. Print the hashtag on the invite, wedding site and program. After the wedding you can go through Twitter, Instagram and Facebook, primarily, and collect all the photos. We then collected all these and shared them into a Tumblr blog, but you can find another method to collect and share them all, if Tumblr's not your thing.

I don't yet recommend ditching the professional photographer for relying primarily on social media, but I think that day is coming. The main reason to keep a pro, I think, is for the wedding party portraits. It's logistically difficult to rely on friends for this task, and you want these photos to come out great. For the rest of the ceremony, however, with an ample number of guests and proper encouragement, I think the day is close at hand where one could get by without professional photographers.

Engagement Portraits

A word about engagement portraits. Engagement portraits are a curious ritual that involves taking cloying, cute photos of you and your future spouse against backdrops of greenery, brick walls, or urban scenes (cityscapes, bridges, farmers markets, and gritty in the streets photos being the most popular of this subset). These are generally taken very early on in this whole engagement process – often even before a wedding date is scheduled. Many people use these for imagery on their save the date cards. They can also be useful if you are vying with your local news publication of record to get your wedding announced in the paper. If you're into that sort of thing. Also, to be fair, families love them.

The planning and execution of these photos is, generally, a separate endeavor from any sort of wedding planning. If you want these, you should plan on doing them very early – indeed, at the outset – of the wedding planning process. I bring them up because they are in fact a very good "trial run" of any photographer you may want to use for the wedding. A serious, on-the-ball planning pro will do their photographer research very, very early in the process, select a potential photographer, and try them out with the engagement photos. Personally, we saw no point to having engagement photos at all, and I didn't have my act together near enough to test a wedding photographer with them. But if these are important to you and you're going to do them, do consider trying to make use of a photographer who's services you are considering procuring for the wedding itself.

An MC

One problem I find with many weddings is that it is not readily apparent when a thing is about to happen. I've missed cake cuttings, first dances, speeches and more because I've been in another room, in the bathroom, or at the bar. There have been times I've simply been oblivious to the fact that something is happening.

To combat this problem, let me introduce you to the concept of the master of ceremonies, or MC. The MC is someone who pre-announces each and every event at the reception. I suppose they could rap, like MC Hammer, but it is not strictly necessary. Just announce things. Time to cut the cake? The MC announces it. Speeches about to begin, let me introduce you to Sarah, the sister of the bride, and the maid of honor. This is doubly useful because many toasting guests actually forget to introduce themselves – hey, they're nervous. It might be their first time.

Many wedding DJs also play the role of MC, if you want it. Talk to any wedding DJ about this possibility, and include the times for their announcements, as well as the words, in your wedding timeline.

Alternatively, you can ask a friend to be the MC. We did this, and it was just great. But either way, do think about the timing and flow of the room, and the acoustics. Make sure everyone can hear the MC, and that they have time to come up from the bathroom in the basement, for example, in time to see the cake cutting.

Wedding Tech

One of the weakest points of traditional wedding planning books is their utter lack of helpful information around technology at weddings. This is the 21st century, and, as famed conehead and investor Marc Andreesen says, "software is eating the world." That is, technology is having a profound impact on all industries. The wedding industry is no different, and it has been undergoing many changes in the last decade brought upon by technology. Many useful tools – some specific to wedding planning, and some not – have cropped up in the last few years. Whereas perhaps five years ago, the sum total of technology brought to bear on the subject of wedding planning might have been the gadgetry your photographer and videographer had and maybe an account at theknot. com, there are now an infinite number of tools to make our lives easier. Let's walk through several of them.

Google

Throughout this book we are going to assume you've heard of and use Google (the search engine) and know how to do your own Google searches. I may occasionally point you to a good Google search, but by and large, I assume you know how to find decent info on things by using the search engine everyone in the world uses (apologies if you are a hard core Bing or DuckDuckGo user). This book isn't a directory of vendors, there are plenty of those on the Internet.

Pinterest

It's conceivable to plan a wedding in the 21st century without Pinterest. It's also conceivable to go without a cell phone, or go to work without hearing about Game of Thrones. For the rest of us, Pinterest is going to be a part of your life for the next few months.

Pinterest, for the uninitiated, is a web platform that allows for the creation, sharing and publishing of visual look boards, or scrapbooks. It is immensely popular, and highly integrated with many of the popular websites on the web through the implementation of a "pin it" button. This button allows users to save an image of, say, a dress or a pair of shoes, from an e-commerce website to your "boards." This makes it easy to share a collection of images or products from many sites and stores with your future spouse, your vendors, family, and anyone else. Users can "follow" boards from other users, getting notifications when there have been changes or additions. Finally, when you follow several boards from several users, your home page then becomes a never-ending stream of imagery from the creators of all the boards you follow.

My first experience with Pinterest was less than ideal. When I first signed up, it was from idle curiosity rather than any specific need to share look books or collections of products. While Pinterest's chief utility lies in the creation of sharing of boards, because of the stream-like view of imagery that is visible on a user's home page, many users use Pinterest in the manner of other social networks like Twitter, Instagram or a Facebook. Pinterest also features an ability to "find your friends" when signing up, allowing you to enter your Facebook credentials and seeing if any of your Facebook friends use Pinterest. You can then follow all your Facebook friends on Pinterest. Pinterest's user base is also heavily female – to the tune of 80% . These features give one the feeling, when you are a man, of making signing up for Pinterest a strange experience. You sign up, add your friends, and are immediately barraged with a never-ending barrage of dresses, shoes, mason jars, farm tables, cookware and hairstyles. It is not immediately apparent why this might be useful to you.

(Pro-tip for men using Pinterest when not-wedding planning. Be selective in who you follow when signing up. When I later went in and unfollowed many of my women friends (sorry), things changed immensely. I also started following boards that were of more interest to me, including some fab boards around musical instruments, computers and the like. I enjoy it now.)

This lack of excitement, however, disappeared immediately when I started planning my wedding. Pinterest is immensely useful in a number of ways for wedding planning. Because you can pin items from e-commerce sites, it makes a great tool for comparison shopping and storing potential items you will need to purchase. When you pin an image to a board, Pinterest maintains a link back to the original product site. This allows you to rapidly build a collection, of, say, affordable ring pillows. You can then send the board to your mate and say "pick one of these." She can pick one from a batch of affordable items, and off you go. Easy as pie.

Pinterest is also useful for mood boards or look boards. You can work with your future spouse and your wedding planner (if you have one) to create a board of visual inspiration for how you want your wedding to look. Often it is difficult to verbally convey a visual feel. Pinterest allows you to describe your desired look and feel visually. Sign up for a Pinterest account early. Make separate boards for visual inspiration, as well as individual items like flowers, decorations, lighting cake decoration and the like.

A warning: in terms of wedding porn, you will never find a more wretched hive of scum and villainy than Pinterest. Shit can get insane. There are some seriously crazy wedding obsessives on Pinterest. You can get sucked in. You can start to feel a keen sense of keeping up with the joneses. Remember the mission. Don't get sucked in.

With some self-control, Pinterest can save huge amounts of time in your planning process, and can rapidly streamline the awkward process of making specific purchase decisions. With any luck you can avoid the existential crisis that ensues from spending hours thinking about napkin rings.

Notetaking

Wedding planning is an exercise in organization, and when it comes to personal organization, few new pieces of software have had as great as an impact as Evernote. Yes, Evernote has competitors, and if you are using one of them (such as Springpad or Simplenote), great. Use that. If you're not, however, download Evernote right now.

Evernote is a note taking app that works on your computer, phone, and tablet, and automatically synchronizes all your notes across all of these devices. It lets you organize your notes into notebooks, by topics and tags. It allows you to take pictures of documents and save them as images and searchable text. This will be immensely useful for you. You will want to start notebooks for various aspects of your wedding – budget, venues, decorations, even documents like contracts. Take copious notes, save all your estimates and documentation into your notes. Get organized and stay organized.

Evernote is also sharable, which means you can grant access to your future spouse and your wedding planner if you are using one, as well as anyone else that may need to see certain notes. Notes can be shared so that people can just see them, or they may be editable by all parties.

If you're a hard-core engineer, consider using one of the project-management suites out there, including Asana and Pivotal Tracker. My friend Morgan works at Pivotal and she says that many people have successfully used Pivotal Tracker for weddings. Hey! Whatever works for you. Use the software you are comfortable with.

Google Docs

Another collaborative software suite that will be immensely useful is Google Docs. Google Docs allows you to create shared and collaborative word processing, spreadsheet and other types of documents. A shared Google spreadsheet will be immensely useful, for example, in building up your guest list. You, your spouse, and anyone else you want to have input on the topic can collaboratively work on the spreadsheet. Include columns for first name, last name, mailing address, email and more so that when the time comes to prepare the actual invitations, you'll have all the information you need.

For both Evernote and Google docs, there exists a robust repository of helpful templates on the web. A simple googling of "Evernote Wedding Templates" and "Google Docs wedding templates" will get you started. Evernote, in particular, has great, helpful content on its blog about the effective use of Evernote for weddings.

Your Wedding Website

No wedding in the 21st century is complete without a wedding website. You'll want to build a simple website that gives guests to the wedding all relevant information about the wedding, including where and when, any information about wedding registries, attire. After the wedding, the wedding website can remain as a permanent memento of the wedding and a central repository for all the photos you will collect on the internet from your guests.

If you know how to make a website, great. If not, two great places to think about starting are Squarespace and Tumblr. Both of these sites allow for the easy creation of websites by people with no coding skills, and have a wide assortment of templates that look good for wedding use. There are an infinite number of other options, including website building applications provided by Google, Apple, Microsoft and more, so if you have one that you are comfortable with, great. If not, Squarespace and Tumblr are a great place to start. You'll want to get a simple site up once you've decided on the date and the venue. You can put up the site with just this information, and add more as you know it and learn it, including information about wedding registries and hotel blocks that are available.

Every wedding needs a good URL. This is the web address for the wedding site. Ours was www.rickandemma.com. This is a common approach – both of your names in the URL. This gives your guests something easy to remember, and helps with Google search engine optimization, so if people can't remember where your website is, they can just google your name. Register your domain name with a domain name provider such as Godaddy (or any other with which you feel comfortable). You'll then need to link your domain name to your website. Squarespace and Tumblr make this very easy, providing instructions on how to handle this. Squarespace also handles domain registration, so it makes a good one-stop destination for all this.

Try not to get too carried away. Mike cautions, "I made a parallax scrolling overproduced site with a custom built RSVP system but honestly just use Squarespace. Be done with it. Even professional designers and developers don't bother these days with making their own sites."

The website should include the time and location of the wedding, reception and other events. It should include a link to any registries. It should include a short blurb about the couple, and a nice photo or two. Most usefully, however, it should include a short "Frequently Answered Questions" section, or FAQ. The single most common question you're going to get about your wedding? "What should I wear?" Have an answer in your FAQ. Is it casual? Formal? Fun? Fancy? Frisky? Something else the starts with F? Let people know. As weddings become more and more varied, people are less sure what they should wear. Help them out! People like to plan in advance.

Remember that no online tool is permanent (remember your Myspace page? Where is it now?) The only way to ensure that your wedding website lasts forever is to incur the expense, in perpetuity, of paying for the hosting yourself. For many people, this is not practical. Just remember that even Tumblr or Squarespace might go out of business one day. Back everything up at home. Make copies.

Twitter

Many people in this modern cyber-era of the future like to have a Twitter hashtag for their wedding. A hashtag is a word that people append to their tweets so that people can follow the hashtag and see things that are going on around it. While this can seem sort of silly to those who aren't on social media, there is one concrete benefit. If you make the hashtag known to all of your guests, savvy guests will use the hashtag when posting to Twitter, Facebook, or Instagram. This will allow you to easily find, after the fact, all the photos your wedding guests took at the wedding.

When choosing a hashtag, be sure that is unique. Go to http://search.twitter.com and type in the hashtag you are considering. Do the same on Instagram. Make sure no one has posted anything using this hash tag in several months, if ever. It can be

Man Nup

extremely confusing if everyone at your wedding is using the hashtag #ourwedding, for example, when millions of other people are as well. It defeats the purpose.

E-Mail Lists

In tandem with your Google doc of wedding guests, I recommend using an emailing program such as Tinyletter to stay in touch with your wedding guests, especially in the early days when you are sending out a save the date announcement. It's easy to export all the names and email addresses from Google docs and import them into an emailing app like Tinyletter. Because many personal email accounts limit the number of people you can send a single email to, if you are having a large wedding, using something like Tinyletter will be a lifesaver, allowing you to easily send emails to everyone invited to the wedding without having to worry about not messing up BCCs or having to send ten separate emails to make sure you stay under the recipient limit in your normal email like Gmail. Tinyletter can also handle responses, and unsubscribes, which makes things easier. As you learn which guests cannot make the event, you can simply unsubscribe them from the list and keep using it for everyone else.

RSVPs

More and more, people are turning to the internet for the process of RSVP handling for weddings. Traditionally, wedding organizers sent out physical invitations to the wedding, which includes a small return card and envelope to let the wedding organizers know if you plan on attending or not. Many services now exist, such as Paperless Post, that allow for this whole process to be handled digitally. Many people, however, worry that moving this entire process to digital loses a touch of class. Other people enjoy the thought of receiving several cards back in the mail from all of their invited guests, and saving them as a memento. The labor-saving benefits, however, can be substantial.

For our part, we did an electronic RSVP using a simple Google Docs form. This worked for 90% of our attendees. A few older attendees, however, had some confusion around using an electronic RSVP system, and we needed to take care of those manually. For the ancillary events, such as the rehearsal dinner and brunch for out-of-towners, we used Paperless Post, which I quite enjoyed using and thoroughly recommend.

Wedding Aps

Recently I was invited to my friend's wedding and the couple sent an email encouraging me to download an iPhone app for their wedding. This was the first I had heard of such things, and I thoroughly enjoyed it. It allowed our hosts to push out timely information to the guests, including maps of the town, and the latest information on hotels. It also allowed wedding guests to chat with one another, and upload photos.

Turns out there are a few companies that do this, and you can have one too. Appy Couple and Weddingpartyapp.com seem to be the most popular. I expect we'll see more and more of this kind of thing in the coming years, and they are worth looking in to. It can be a fun way to communicate with your guests, and have them communicate with each other.

Lover.ly

One wedding-specific site I want to point out to you is Lover.ly, which has been growing in popularity these last few years. Full disclosure: I am an investor in Lover.ly. I made the investment unrelated to my own wedding planning, but the timing proved fortuitous, as I ended up making use of the product for my own wedding. Lover.ly is a site for wedding inspiration. It allows users to find great imagery, save favorites and share them with their wedding support system – vendors, friends and family. The site curates the best and most beautiful wedding imagery from the industry's top bridal bloggers and combines this with data (color, theme, what have you) so you can browse more effectively, and find what you're looking for in the real world. Loverly makes tackling the granular details of the wedding day less overwhelming. They help couples reflect on why they're tying the knot in the first place and brainstorm ways to make their day one of a kind.

Like Pinterest, Loverly is primarily geared towards woman, but the site endeavors to give both brides and grooms the tools and well-rounded support to help them plan their weddings. Check it out.

Registries

Wedding registries have moved almost completely online in the last few years. It's also not uncommon to pick multiple wedding registries. Choose a few online, and then put the links to them on your wedding site that you made in Squarespace, Tumblr or whatever. It's not uncommon to have a "traditional" wedding registry at some place like Crate & Barrel, Macy's or the like, and a more "fun" one. We recently attended a wedding where one of the registries was at Toys "R" Us. We're also seeing more and more people forgo wedding registries for charity donations (this is the approach we took), which are also usually easy to do online.

There do exist a few tech startups that allow you to compile multiple registries into one, such as MyRegistry.com. I don't see the need for using one of these – it's easier just to make multiple registries.

Day-Of Tech

As any event planner can tell you, technology can be quirky. When planning the technology for the day of your wedding, make sure that there are ample plans for handing any malfunctions and failures. Dedicated staff should be assigned to things like lighting, DJ equipment, public address systems, photography and the like. Handing a piece of technology to a friend and saying "you're in charge of this," will quite likely end in failure, especially since there may well be ample alcohol involved.

We've seen people do some interesting things with technology at the weddings – interactive photo booths, drone flyovers, stop motion videos. We had mixed luck with these, and the learnings fell exactly along the lines I am laying out here. Our digital photo booth was manned by a professional, a friend that we paid as a vendor who brought along staff. It worked perfectly, and we cherish those photos. We also tried to borrow a expensive video camera (the first Red

Epic off the line, if you're a camera nerd) from a friend to do a time-lapse shoot, but since we didn't pay a professional, we got... well, we got nothing. The setup didn't work at all. You get what you pay for. You will have plenty to worry about on your wedding day, and should not be worried about whether the photo booth or DJ has broken down. Find people who are dedicated to the tasks, and get out of their way.

Chapter 9: Looking Good

Wedding Dress

The interplay between men planning weddings and the selection of the bride's wedding dress isn't fully explored. It's undiscovered country. In reading traditional, female-focused wedding planning books, there's not a lot of discussion about the men when choosing the wedding dress. But as you are planning the wedding, you'll need to figure out how to be useful, and keep things on track, without being too controlling about a topic that, by nature, is only peripherally related to you.

The wedding dress isn't a thing you can go and buy for your bride. At best, you can gamely accompany your betrothed on a journey fraught with emotional peril as they grapple with their hopes, dreams, long-dormant childhood fantasies, existential questions about femininity and the meaning of the color white (blame Queen Victoria – she's the one who popularized the color. Before her, wedding dresses were all sorts of colors). And that's the best of cases. I'm really not trying to imply that women are neurotic. I don't blame them. The whole concept is, *prima facie,* kinda screwy. First off, it's expensive as hell − needlessly so. You pay an arm and a leg for something you're only going to use once. Then there are all the very real concerns about being judged solely on your looks, which − let's face it − sucks. Any right-thinking person would find the whole situation somewhat appalling. "Oh, let me go spend potentially thousands of dollars on a thing that will only get me judged, then head to the waste bin." Yeah, sign me up.

Any person who loves their significant other would rightly feel an urge to help someone out when they're confronted when faced with such ghastly circumstances. Thus it will hurt to hear that there's only so much you can do.

The good news is that there are *some* things you can do. Should she need it, you can help in the same manner that you do when the two of you are out shopping, or when she's getting ready for a cocktail party. You can sit patiently and say you like this part of that dress. You can take part in long conversations about whether it's appropriate to wear white to weddings in this day and age, and how cool it is that the Chinese get to wear red. We can also tell our bride that they don't need to spend a bunch of money. We can reassure them that we love them as they are, they are beautiful, and you are totally okay with it if they want to spend $10 on a dress off of eBay and be done with it. Never bat an eye. Never deviate from this message. It will probably only help 10 or 20 percent, but it's absolutely worth saying. It should have the added benefit of being true, because, honestly, what's wrong with you if it's not?

If you're blessed with wealth, be warned: open-ended budgets on wedding dress shopping can be tyranny. It can seem like it would be quite helpful not being bound by fiduciary constraints, yet in fact quite the opposite turns out to be true. Like all things wedding planning related, you'll probably go over your budget a smidge (remember the 5% guideline in making your overall budget). But knowing that you absolutely cannot go over, for example, $1,000 puts whole groups of dresses and whole designer lines out of your spouse's reach, and shuts down whole lines of paranoid inquiry. She might buy an $1100 dress, but having a budget number will keep her from looking too hard at the ten thousand dollar dresses. There is freedom in constraints.

Have a frank conversation with your future spouse about how much you both feel comfortable spending – and stick to it. And above all, remember that that number can be as low as you want. There is no shame.

There will be times she will freak out. This is to be expected. When this happens, offer emotional support, and try not to escalate the situation. There are probably going to be times where some incomprehensible fashion accessory or dress part is causing massive emotional distress and it will literally make no sense to you. You might not even understand the actual physics of the problem. Be supportive. Be understanding. It's a monumentally stressful situation. Some women find the idea of getting up in front of everyone they know and being judged on their looks as rather terrifying. Honestly, that seems perfectly understandable. Beyond these things, you can but get out of the way. If you are artful and talented at offering sartorial advice, you can venture to do so to the level you're traditionally comfortable commenting on your mate's fashion choices. Unfortunately, even this is only mildly useful.

Do remember that luckily there's a good chance she won't need your help at all. Unlike when the two of you are at home getting ready for a big night out, in this situation she has at least one other person – her maid of honor – and potentially several others, who are all too willing to help.

For this is, for better or worse, a job for the bridesmaids. You may find this comforting. For my part it was nice to know good friends had my wife's back, and that she was in good hands. In our case, Emma decided that the dress was going to be her financial contribution to the wedding, so I didn't even need to worry about the budget. I did, however, do my best to reassure her that I supported any of her decisions, and she need not spend any money. We briefly considered spending an insane amount of money on something she saw in a bridal magazine, but thankfully that period was mercifully short.

We pause here to acknowledge that ancient custom of the groom not seeing the bride on their wedding day. Origins are once again murky, but a quick Googling gives you the general gist: it had to do with brides as property, arranged marriages and the like. Yeeaah. I'll bet that's right up your alley. Recently I was chatting with some friends who were sticking to this custom, and it did seem kind of fun, but he wasn't planning the wedding. I should also point out that this hallowed tradition makes impossible one of my favorite wedding tricks: to get the wedding portraits out of the way prior to the ceremony. If you are going this route, however, there's even *less* you can do to help your bride. So, one less thing on your plate I suppose?

As in all things nuptial, time is of the essence here. Brides may have doubts. Brides may change minds. Sometimes they purchase a dress, return it, purchase another one. If this needs to happen for your future spouse to feel good about their dress, so be it. You can help carve out the time to make it happen. Also take care to include time for alterations, because they will freakin' ream you if you have to do a rush job. It won't do to encourage your bride to choose a dress based on a particular store's policy around alterations and refunds, but definitely make note of them, keep track, and mark down relevant dates in your calendar.

Wedding dresses are a bit like mattresses, difficult to comparison shop due to numerous model numbers/SKUs for the same dress (shout out to the mattress company Caper – six mattress models – one for each size mattress. Someone do the same for wedding dresses?) Nonetheless the endeavor is worth it, and deals can be had online and with last year's designs. These are worth exploring, as are consignment shops, sample sales and the like. But any competent shopper knows these tricks – most of them apply to wedding dresses as they do to any nice dress.

Finally, here's a shout out to "the nice dress." Buying a gorgeous non-wedding cocktail dress your future wife can use another day? Kismet.

Bridal Salons

We should probably also warn you about bridal salons. A bridal salon is a wedding dress store on steroids: part high-end retail establishment, part tailor, part lobby of the Four Seasons, part ladies-who-lunch tea salon. They are no place for a man. Avoid these places. Thank your lucky stars if your bride is keen to avoid them too. Much like modern hotels and retail establishments have signature scents or music playlists, bridal salons have signature voodoo. There is some magic in the air at these places, and between the time you choose the dress and the time you walk out the door, you will have magically incurred another 20-30% of the cost of the dress in fees. Garters. Lingerie. Shoes. These things add up.

Bridal salons are actually kind of amazing and surreal. Unlike any other niche of the American retail experience. But they are not your friend. These are the province of brides, maids of honor, bridesmaids and family. If you are getting cajoled, play the tradition card and get out. If you *have* to go, bring your phone, take some pictures of the place and send them to me. I've always wanted to see inside of one besides Priscilla of Boston, to which I once made a delivery in my college years.

My wife, luckily, shared many of these opinions, but did make a trip to David's Bridal, where she eventually chose a lovely dress with the help of her bridesmaid. This was her second dress, after she had attempted to have something custom made in China on the cheap, which did not work out. I wonder what happened with that dress. Once she chose the dress, it didn't arrive for another week. This, coupled with the original, abortive attempt, leads me to advise that as the wedding planner you should keep your bride on schedule, and have her go in early. Don't procrastinate.

Shoes

A wedding dress must (simply must, dahling) have shoes to match. Choose the dress, then find shoes to match is the order of the day, with the additional option of buying slippers that you then dye to match the dress. Online outlets often sell wedding shoes in hues matching popular dresses – there are several places that make custom hues to match any dress color. My wife ended up buying and trying several pairs of shoes and wearing different shoes throughout the night. Your bride will probably do this as well. Buying a good base pair of dyed-to-match shoes just to have is a good idea even though in the end she may end up choosing a pair of pumps or heels she already owns.

Also, though this is advice for the bride, we will pass it on here: remember that you can change your shoes, and your dress may well cover the shoes you wear during the ceremony. If you're not a fan of heels, this can be a blessing: you can wear wedding slippers under the dress and no one will be the wiser.

Undergarments

Let's talk about lingerie. Any excuse for men to talk about lingerie, right? Because we sit around and talk about lingerie *all the time.*

Some practical advice to pass along to your bride: feel free to not go "full bridal," and simply wear something nice that can be reused. Romantic, right? Or, perhaps, you want her to go full tilt. White furry poofy bras, garters, the whole kit and caboodle. I had one friend who not only went this route, but joined her entire wedding party in the post-reception suite late night party in her full bridal lingerie get up. Hear hear, I say. But, I mean, really, this is up to her. It isn't your domain unless it's something you and your better half are already in the habit of doing.

It's traditional for a groom to give his future spouse a little gift, and not unheard of to make that gift lingerie. You can consider this, but I find jewelry to be a classier choice. At any rate, there's a good chance she'll receive some wedding lingerie from the shower.

This is a horrible, awkward tradition where a bride wears a garter and the groom throws it out into the audience at the reception and some dude is supposed to catch it and that dude's supposed to get married later, and honestly, it's a pretty iffy tradition. But if your wedding has a theme where this could work, you will need a garter. Buy it online, for cheap. You could get one on Amazon. I mean, you're just going to throw it away. They rarely intentionally match the dress, as they're not seen. But, really, just don't. No one misses it.

Veil and Headpiece

Many brides choose to wear wedding veils, or it's simpler stepsister, a headpiece. The wedding veil has a long and strange history. Ancient Roman brides wore flame-colored veils, called *flammeum*, to protect them from evil spirits. In Judaism, the use of the veil goes back to Genesis 24:65 in the Torah, where Rebekah is brought to Isaac by her father Abraham's servant. In the more recent era, the veil assisted in keeping the prying eyes of the groom from seeing his new bride. Because we thought that was a good idea at some point in human history. In the western tradition, a veil symbolizes virginity, because virginal brides wore their hair down on their wedding day, and the veil was a representation of that. This brought forth the rather weird tradition where the father lifted the veil and presented the bride to the groom. This still happens, though we also now have the groom do the job himself, or forgo the custom entirely.

The point here is that there is a lot of religious baggage around the veil, which may or may not be important to you spiritually. You and your betrothed should do what's comfortable and she should wear what's comfortable, adopting specific religious practices as you see fit. You should have these discussions with your spouse-to-be, but defer to her judgement.

Just putting this out there: the headpiece is a more modern contraption, designed to maintain some of the spirit of the veil without all of the religious baggage.

Jewelry

Your spouse will want to accessorize her outfit with jewelry. Two points to note here relevant to you: first, there is a tradition where you buy your betrothed a gift prior to the wedding. This is often jewelry. To reinforce this, many traditional wedding planning books – which your future spouse may be reading at this very moment – also point out that there's a good chance that for this gift, you'll be buying them a piece of jewelry. It is indeed the most common choice. She may, therefore, be assuming you're going to buy jewelry, and thus not pick out jewelry for her outfit. What an embarrassing mixup! Oh la la! To avoid this, you may want to go ahead and bow to tradition and buy her some jewelry. Failing that, at least let her know if you don't plan to.

Something Borrowed...

Secondly, jewelry is an important part of the "something borrowed something blue, something old, something new" adage. If your family has some family heirloom in the form of jewels, it is perhaps worth considering letting your future spouse wear this, in order to fulfill the "something borrowed" component of this tradition. I mean, it's a lot more hygienic than borrowed lingerie. I didn't just say that.

The fun of this tradition is that the bulk of it happens spontaneously. People plot, gifts are proffered at the last minute. If you're *super* into planning, you can have a couple things at the ready that will make nice, small, romantic additions to the attire to fulfill the tradition. But do be aware a parent, grandparent, or best friend might have something to offer as well. But, geez. I really like this tradition. So cute, so dada.

Hair and Makeup

In terms of hair and makeup, here you can be a bit more helpful. This requires a vendor. Your future spouse may or may not already have vendors lined up. If not, you can prove somewhat helpful by using your magic vendor-finding powers and doing the research on potential vendors who suit your needs. You can handle the negotiations and the payment. You can handle the scheduling. Do what you can.

Stylists and make up artists come to you on the day of the event. You may want to get one for your fiancé and one for the bridesmaids, as this is one of the most time-consuming components of the morning pre-wedding preparations. Ask the hair stylist for a timing schedule, and make sure they know how many people are in the wedding party that will be getting their hair done. Include the mother in all of this and any other female members of the wedding party. As ever, plan well in advance, as the good ones book up early.

Hair stylists are not cheap. And it's hard to go budget on this. You can consider saving some money by using a friend, or the having the wedding party do it themselves, but these aren't really your decisions to make as a planner. Get estimates early to factor into your budget. If your betrothed has a favorite stylist, check their availability as soon as you have your date locked down.

Bridesmaids' Dresses

It's really none of my business – or our business as grooms – to get too involved in this, but nonetheless I feel I must take a bit of a stand on behalf of women. For the love of god, try and avoid making your bridesmaids all wear ridiculously expensive, ugly-as-hell matching dresses. It doesn't work. Pick an easy color, some guidelines, and let them wear what they want. We chose black. It looked quite lovely, and they matched the groomsmen. Women come in all shapes and sizes, and different styles and cuts look better on different women. Why would you want to make a bunch of your best friends suffer needlessly? Then there's the economic impact of having to shell out a bunch of money for a dress you'll never wear again (if you're paying for your wife's dress you already know this pain).

This is, however, going to be the bride's domain, so there's only so much you can do. And, you know, some people have childhood dreams wrapped up in their wedding, and need things just-so. Try to do what you can on behalf of your bridesmaids and help your future wife maintain some perspective. Express sympathy if they end up having to buy a throw-away lilac taffeta gown for $400, and say thank you a million times. Beyond that, it's out of your hands.

Men's Clothing

Men. Fashion. It's a pickle. Since time immemorial, men's formal fashion has pretty much been a suit. The specifics of any given generation vary – whether the "norm" is a tuxedo, with or without or tails, bow tie or cravat, top hat or no – but really at any given time, there was "one right answer." In this modern age, things are a bit more... messy. Ours is an age of cultural, stylistic and historical sampling and remixing. Not only do we have all of human history at our fingertips, but we live in an era where personal expression is allowed, and increased leeway has been given to men in what constitutes acceptable clothing.

This is a blessing and a curse. Your father didn't have to think much about what he was going to wear to his wedding. It was a suit or a tux, depending on whether it was black tie or not. End of story. Some people my find such lack of choice refreshing and reassuring (Loki to Director Fury: "Freedom is life's great lie.") Others may find it stifling. The good thing is that if you DO find an overabundance of choice terrifying, you can still totally wear a suit or a tux and call it a day. How super is that?

Indeed, that's how I am. I don't like variety in my fashion. So I kept things pretty straightforward: I wore a black tux, a vest, a white tux shirt, and a bow tie. I told my grooms to wear a black suit and white shirt, and that I'd get them matching ties, and to let me know whether they wanted bow, straight, or skinny straight. In a nod to my wife, I had the bow ties match the color of her dress. Because, yes, the wedding industrial complex is such that you can literally buy bow ties custom dyed to match the color of popular wedding dresses (in my case "Vera Wang for David's Bridal Blush"). I bought the bow ties for the best man and groomsmen, as many of them did not rank "owning a blush bow tie" high on their bucket list.

Those bow tie stores are pretty crazy, by the way. There are several on the web, and they may well blow your mind if you've never delved into this particular word of sartorial manliness. And, a year later, I still was still getting junk mail from them. I guess they're hoping the marriage won't last or something. They even updated my address when I switched cities. Hell, I moved to a different state, and here it is, two years later. I am still getting catalogs from The Beau Tie.

Now, some men like fashion. Go for it. I've gone to weddings where my friends have gone full tilt: bespoke, custom suits. One wore a denim suit and that was amazing. Kilts. Top hats. Tails. You name it. If you can dream it you can wear it. Welcome to 21st century America. There is one constraint, however, and that is your future spouse. You should include him/her in these decisions. If you're thinking of doing something wacky, absolutely consult your better half. And if you're planning on some joint themed matching outfits, that's some next level shit right there, and I cannot advise you, because you clearly have a vision.

So good on you. Go for it. It's your big day. Do what you want.

Some practical advice for those pursuing a vision: getting things custom made – such as a bespoke suit – is not only expensive but time consuming. Start early. It's easy to mock those women who start a Pinterest wedding board before they're engaged but you know what? They have a plan. Planning is good. There is money to be saved by using overseas tailors – especially in Hong Kong – but these take time. You want ample time to go through two to three rounds of revisions or re-dos. If you live in a city where there exists a robust industry of local bespoke men's tailors, great. Do be aware that even then, things will take time (though time will be saved by you being able to come in for fittings). And local manufacturer is almost certainly more expensive.

Ryan brings up a good point about the joys of bespoke clothing for larger men. "I'm huge. I look like you should be asking me three questions to cross an old wooden bridge. Consequently, the average off-the-rack suits and tuxedos don't fit me. Even with the most extreme tailoring, the most excessive shaving away of titanic swaths of fabric, I still resemble a 6-year-old's drawing of his father on the way to work. Luckily there's been a surge of affordable, fully-custom men's clothing companies springing up online recently, and this is where I solved my wedding tuxedo problem. I would highly recommend this approach unless you're built, inexplicably, like a John Varvatos model. For a surprisingly reasonable price and very little fiddling around with tape measures, I obtained a three piece tuxedo for under a thousand dollars that not only made me look like a real grown up at my own wedding, but will continue to look good on me for subsequent events in my future, whatever they might be. Suits that fit well just look better. Suits that fit perfectly make you look like James Bond. The bride will collect more compliments than the man standing next to her in a tuxedo. But you will look and feel a lot better in your own, perfectly tailored armor. And someday you might find yourself at a black tie event standing next to a guy wearing a tuxedo that doesn't fit any better than the day he wore it at his wedding. You will feel politely superior."

If you're on a budget, wear a suit you own already, or invest in a simple, normal suit that you can re-use. It's good to own one suit, and there's no major reason, these days, you can't just get married wearing a normal suit. Hit up someplace like Men's Warehouse or Filene's Basement to find a good deal. Honestly, a cheap suit is fine. The secret is to invest in some tailoring and get it to fit right, and have the suit, tie and shirt all match. You can save money by buying a nice shirt and tie and using the suit you have. Have your future spouse, your best man, or even the salesman at the store help you find an elegant and affordable combination.

Man Nup

Chapter 10: Events Not On Your Wedding Day

Engagement Party

Many couples like to have an engagement party not long after they've been engaged. This is traditionally hosted by the bride's parents, but hey – anything goes. As far as I can tell, the purpose of this is mainly for the family, to provide closure to a parent in some circle-of-life emotional thing about "wow my daughter is all grown up and now she is getting married and I just remember when she was a little girl." Come to think of it, that's gotta be a pretty amazing feeling. I will check my cynicism. Obviously, if your better half's mother wants to plan this, then let 'er rip – not much you have to do. If she doesn't, there's no real obligation to do this unless you and/ or your future spouse are into it. We didn't do one. If you do want to do one, and you can't rely on your future spouse's mother, you might consider asking your own mother to do this, or perhaps just organize one yourself. This seems to be a more and more common thing – people just have a bunch of people over at a bar or something. While this, historically and traditionally, could be a somewhat fancy affair, especially in the cities, nowadays it can be a casual fun thing. No need to go crazy over it.

I do find that the engagement party is a nice balm for expensive destination weddings, since many people may not be able to attend.

Showers

It's a brave man who plans a wedding. It's a braver man still who plans a bridal shower. If you can leave these tasks to the bridesmaids and maid of honor, great. To lessen the burden, it's good if you offer to pay for the event, and/or find a venue for the event. Some bridesmaids will approach their task with relish and politely rebuff your offers. Some will be quietly thankful and take you up on it. Let them maintain the appearance of being the planning lead, but if you can help, do. Occasionally brides have multiple showers – often one organized by the maid of honor and one organized by the mother of the bride.

Rehearsal

Schedule it. Plan it. Figure out when it is, in advance, and let your wedding party know as soon as you can. If you're doing a Saturday wedding, for example, and the rehearsal is on Friday, that's a whole different level of travel arrangements for people, and they will need to know. It's common for people to hold the rehearsal on the same day of the wedding precisely because of the travel situation, with the rehearsal dinner the night before (it's okay – logically it makes no sense but people just roll with it). I am not personally a fan of this. You're going to have enough to do the day of your wedding, better to get this out of the way in advance.

There's a good chance that one or more of the wedding party won't be able to make it to the rehearsal if you're doing a Saturday wedding and told them about the rehearsal rather late and they can't take up an extra day of vacation at work. That's okay. One or two people missing will be fine. Other people will help them out.

Of equal importance is working out the rehearsal with the venue, and the wedding planner, if you have one. Many venues and planners are doing many, many weddings during the busy season. They may have a wedding the day before yours, or even another one the same day. Make sure you get this scheduled. If you have a wedding planner, it's especially important that they be there, or at least their assistant.

This is also a place where a wedding planner can come in quite useful. Up until this moment, you've not spent much time planning how the actual music playing, procession, readings and the rest is going to go down. And people will need instructions. They will also need someone to guide them the next day, telling them exactly when to walk, what to do, where to stand. People's emotions get in the way of their common sense on wedding days, and the calm, instructional tone of your planner will be vital.

Rehearsal Dinner

The rehearsal dinner is traditionally put on by the groom's parents so, you know, explore that avenue first. If your parents are into it, the thing to do here is handle the planning yourself and just give them the bill, thus maintaining your vice-like grip over all aspects of wedding planning like the good control freak that you are. More practically, doing this will keep you from having to have last-minute arguments with your mother about the menu, and avoiding long, existential conversations about why so many people these days are vegan or gluten free. Planning it yourself may add a smidge of hassle to your life, though compared to the work you've already taken it's a trifle, and the benefits are real.

The whole thing can add up financially. You're basically buying dinner for 20-30 people, and a nice dinner at that. Look for prix fixe menu options, preset menus. Private dining rooms at nice restaurants can be quite nice, as can someone's home, if you have a friend that just loves entertaining. You don't want to undertake this yourself – you'll have other things on your mind. When inspecting the room, take care to make sure that it's not too loud of a room – the conversation of 20 people can really bounce off those artisanal stone walls. Slowly everyone speaks up to adjust, and the whole thing ascends in a deafening spiral that is rather unpleasant to your elderly attendees. Look for fabric on the walls or something like that. That's a pro tip, right there.

Many restaurants specialize in this sort of thing and offer all sorts of add-ons. Booze, top shelf booze, better wine and the like are potential add-ons, and probably worth shelling out for. There are often also paid options for flowers, nicer furniture, artesian birch branch centerpieces and the like. I find these unnecessary. Pick a nice place, take the room as is. The rehearsal dinner does not need to be an epic, ostentatious affair. Semi-casual is totally fine.

The rehearsal dinner is attended by, typically, the families and the bridal party. Accommodate their spouses or significant others. If you have readers, ushers, ring bearers, officiants, or any other extended wedding party members, it's good to invite them as well, since, well, there will be a rehearsal preceding the dinner, and you'll probably want them to be there. A nice dinner is like the carrot that gets them to the rehearsal itself.

Then there are the toasts. This is curious. Toasts, now, are actually in two places: the rehearsal dinner and the reception. Figure out who's doing what in which place. Some people may do two. The groom's family typically does the first toast at the rehearsal dinner, especially if they're paying. If you want a few other people to, great. These toasts are more casual than the toasts at the reception. If someone's doing two, give 'em a little coaching so they don't use up all their best material at the rehearsal dinner.

The Night Before

Some people like to do a little something the night before the wedding. This is especially common if you have a lot of out-of-towners. We did an out-of-towner's drinks the night before the wedding, right after the rehearsal dinner. This is a nice thing to do because sometimes these people have no idea what to do in the town you've brought them to. It doesn't have to go too late, and it doesn't have to be too fancy. We just booked a back room at a bar. A friend of mine once offered hay rides at a farm not far from her childhood home. None of her friends had been there before, and it was fun to get a sense of local color and local wine. The wine helped a lot. It was quite pleasant. The presence of you and your betrothed doesn't have to be too extended at this event: remember it's important that you get your sleep. You can pop in and say hi, hang out an hour two, and go home. The nice thing is that you're just giving everyone a thing to do and a place to go. Even if you don't have the exact location worked out it's good to have this scheduled in advance when you send out the invitations so people can plan their travel around it.

Post Wedding Brunch

Along the same lines of the pre-wedding drinks, another add-on option is to have a brunch the afternoon of the day after the wedding. This one's a bit more traditional and is often hosted by a family member. It's a convenient flourish to offer up to a family member to host if you have an extra one. Also, it's nice to have an activity for the out-of-towner's to do. You may well have been out late for your wedding, so take care to not schedule this too too early, you'll need your beauty sleep. It's good to let people know when this thing starts and show up at that time, because a lot of people may be just popping in and saying hi before they hit the road, and it can be disappointing if you're not there. If you think you're going to be late, just schedule it later. Like the pre-wedding drinks, it's good to have this scheduled in advance and mentioned somewhere in the invitation or on the website, so people can plan around it.

Honeymoons

This isn't a honeymoon planning book, but a few words here: throughout this whole wedding process, if you're a traditionalist couple and you've elected to have a honeymoon immediately after the wedding, you and your better half will also be confronted with the tasks of planning the honeymoon. This is more work. Consider either postponing the honeymoon planning until after the wedding, or, if you really want to do it right now, breaking up the planning duties between you and your partner on this one. If you do elect to do all the planning of a honeymoon immediately following the wedding, consider hiring a travel agent. They can help. If this is too expensive, or you want to go it alone, then go for it. No fear. If you're like most people, you have more experience planning a nice trip than a wedding, so you might be able to pull it off without too much fuss. In planning the transportation for the wedding, if you're doing the whole "immediately set off for the honeymoon" thing, make sure to account for it in your booking of limos.

Bachelor Parties

Bachelor parties are also strange for the mix of people. It's not uncommon to bring more of your friends than just the groomsmen. This has its pros and cons if everyone isn't a good friend already. When your groomsmen don't already know each other, a bachelor party of just you and the groomsmen is a useful bonding experience to help them get to know one another and feel comfortable before the wedding. When there's a larger group, more fun might be had, but if one of them doesn't know everyone else, they may feel isolated. Curate your attendees so that everyone's got someone they're buddies with, or it's a small enough group for forced bonding.

The Date

Back when men were men and the rivers ran with whiskey, the bachelor party served a real purpose. It was the night before the wedding. It was a ritual designed to get the future husband completely s**t-faced, and, thus, monumentally hung over, ergo, pliable. A hung over groom is a docile groom. They'll do and say what they need to to get through the whole ordeal. Whether this ritual was more disrespectful to brides or grooms it is difficult to say, so perhaps this is a tradition best consigned to history's dustheap.

In this day and age of a civilized man actually thinking about things, people tend to pick a date a month or two in advance of the wedding. In a concretely practical matter, this means that you'll have to have your best man chosen and informed of his duties far enough in advance to take up the cause of planning, if you're charging him with this. You'll also want to take care to choose a date that most people can make, avoiding other people's weddings and other big events.

Vegas

Vegas is a strange place. The Las Vegan (yes, that's the term) powers-that-be have spent a good deal of time and money trying to convince us that Vegas is a family-friendly destination. This is now – thanks to the efforts of misguided investment bankers and the overweight casino titans whom they back – more or less true.

Sort of. In truth, Vegas has not in fact become a family friendly kidz zone, but rather it has added a family-friendly option. Vegas accepts all, and has thus added mom to the long list of constituents to whom the town will cater. For the old Vegas is still there, and if you want to find it, no sweat. Just set foot out onto the Strip any time of day or night, wave your hand, and grasp a single flyer shoved into it by one of the army of pamphleteers before you. Call the number on the flyer. Welcome to a the seedy underbelly of Vegas. Even easier than finding a good Pad Thai recipe with Google. But a lot more expensive.

This makes Vegas an interesting option for a bachelor party, because – hey. Anything goes. The philosopher in me disputes this notion. You can't kill a drifter or engage in nuclear war. But the options for decadent pursuits are somewhat widened from that of a traditional city, amplified by the social atmosphere that does not so readily eschew such transgressive peccadilloes.

There's another benefit that Vegas's donning of a family-friendly image offers the groom-to-be. The veneer of respectability that has been recently painted over the city makes it far more socially acceptable to announce a Vegas bachelor party. There exists now a plausible deniability that did not previously exist (if you're a strip club aficionado looking for such plausible deniability, by the by, it's also worth checking out Portland, Oregon). This can be useful.

It should also be said, however, that Vegas can present some complications. Ever since the internet came and emasculated us all, fewer men are bonded with their male counterparts over severely taboo hobbies such as boning prostitutes, prodigious cocaine consumption, high stakes poker or strip clubs. We tend to meet and make our male friends over more pedestrian pursuits and confine our less socially-acceptable avocations to the anonymous safety of cyberspace. This can mean that, upon arrival in Vegas, we may discover that Bob from accounting has a thing that we really didn't want to know about for

50 year old prostitutes in PVC catsuits. More dangerously, a bachelor party in Vegas that is planned by our best man requires a deep friendship and understanding that many men don't have. If you're not comfortable with such things, it can be profoundly awkward if your best man buys you a hooker on your first night in Vegas, never mind the amount of explaining you may feel compelled to undergo with your future spouse. If you plan a Vegas bachelor party, make your comfort limits known. There's something about Vegas that makes some men endeavor to indulge their vices with relish – on a level at which they would never partake at home. Take care to not accidentally find yourself in a situation with which you're uncomfortable.

All that being said, Vegas is about the money. "The amount of fun you have in Vegas is directly proportional to how much money you spend. It's sad but true," says Mike, who did the Vegas trip. "You want to have a good time at a club? Buy a table. Not just that but buy a table and tip the guy seating you so you get a better table. Then you have to buy bottles of alcohol. Etc. Etc. It's terrible but that's how it goes."

Strippers and Strip Clubs

Strip clubs, too, can provide a mighty good time, if you find such things enjoyable, but are also potentially problematic depending on your relationship with your future spouse. Discussions are best had in advance. Also be aware that there are some areas of obfuscation here, which you may use to your advantage or make a point of clarifying as your own relationship dictates. Specifically I find that for many women, their mate attending a strip club is one thing, but receiving a lap dance is quite another. And it's quite another to hit the town with the strippers afterwards and end up at Tao nightclub or Denny's. Just saying. As in all things I recommend open communication, but this is a wedding planning book, not a relationship guide, so use your best judgement.

A tactical recommendation from wedding planning man Mike: "Do the pro move and call them [the strip club] ahead of time and ask for their limo to pick you up. It gives you free admission and a reserved table."

One practice I would personally caution against is the hired stripper in hotel room. Boy, that can get awkward. This is another area – especially if it happens in Vegas – where the different partaking propensities and views on vice amongst your man-friends can cause some sketchy situations for those who are not stripper-inclined. At least in a club, you can clap along and add your tips without worrying that they're going to climb on top of your prostrate body and shake their moneymaker two inches from your nose. Probably. Unless you have friends who like to pay extra for that sort of thing.

If you do have friends who like to pay extra for that sort of thing, it's best to make your boundaries known in advance. I've found that the "they made me do it and it would have been rude to say no" defense does not go over too well at home for some people. Your mileage may vary.

Who to Bring

Bachelor parties are also strange for the mix of people. It's not uncommon to bring more of your friends than just the groomsmen. This has its pros and cons if everyone isn't a good friend already. When your groomsmen don't already know each other, a bachelor party of just you and the groomsmen is a useful bonding experience to help them get to know one another and feel comfortable before the wedding. When there's a larger group, more fun might be had, but if one of them doesn't know everyone else, they may feel isolated. Curate your attendees so that everyone's got someone they're buddies with, or it's a small enough group for forced bonding.

Bachelor Bachelorette

For couples that have been together a while,

and have a lot of mutual friends, a bachelor-bachelorette party can be a great time. It's a good idea to have one day where each member of the couple's bridesmaids and groomsmen split up and do a separate activity, allowing for some better bonding time. If you go this route, you can plan the details of the main party yourself and have the maid of honor and the best man plan the activities of the solo day and evening where the group splits up into two.

A house rental from Airbnb or VRBO or something can be a great way to have the whole group spend some quality time before the wedding and get to know each other. Choosing the guests for a bachelor-bachelorette party takes a little more care, as you may need to think about significant others and spouses of the bridal party, growing the group to a larger group than it would be if you did the parties individually. Definitely keep this in mind if you are, generously and unnecessarily according to tradition, footing the bill.

I find combined bachelor-bachelorette parties to be enjoyable, especially as I get older. It's a very different sort of holiday weekend than a bachelor party, generally far less debauched (though I suppose your results may vary depending on your friend group), more relaxed. It's also a great option when a lot of people have kids.

A Final Note

Bachelor parties need not be debauched orgies of excess. I've attended several quite pleasant, relaxed bachelor parties that involve cabins in the woods, camping, resorts and the like. As I get older, I really have come to appreciate these, and they do allow for some quality time with your best mates.

Chapter 11: The Ceremony

Here We Go

A big day, indeed. You're going to want to enjoy this day, and you're going to want to remember it. One of the biggest benefits of solid wedding planning is that every detail has been taken care of, in advance, so that you can enjoy your day. This is the goal.

The Assistant

If you've hired a wedding planner that's been with you the whole way, or a week-of/day-of wedding planner, you have this covered. If not, you need to designate someone. You – and your spouse – need help on the big day. Your spouse has her maid of honor. You have your best man, yes, but this is something different. Since you're doing the wedding planning, you're the one that's going to be responsible for all of the decisions made that day – when to bring out the cake, when to start the toasts – unless you designate someone.

Find someone you trust, and have them commit to making sure the itinerary is followed, throughout the whole day and night. From hours before the ceremony until the reception is finished. They should be dedicated to this task. Every time something happens on your wedding itinerary, they should be running over to make sure it's happening.

This is, obviously, a lot of work, and makes it hard for the assistant to enjoy the evening. This is why you can't do it yourself, and why it's often a good idea to get a day-of planner. You want one person you can talk to that will make everything happen, and only one person who will talk to you if there's a planning emergency – and hopefully they won't have to do that at all. If choosing a friend, make sure they know what the situation is, and know they are basically going to be working that night. Find a way to make it up to them.

The Program

We've talked about the design of the wedding program, but you'll also need to, well, write it. This is a document you hand out to everyone at the wedding letting them know what's going to go down during the ceremony. You should list the members of the wedding party – bridesmaids, groomsmen, ring bearers, flower children, officiant, ushers, family of the couple. You should also list out the order that things are going to happen. Writing this document is a good exercise for visualizing how the ceremony will progress. Typically this includes opening words from the officiant, some readings or musical performances, exchanging of the vows from the couple, and the actual exchanging of rings and vows presided over by the officiant (sometimes these two things are one in the same, sometimes they are separate). You should also list the processional and recessional, and mention what music is being played. You'll obviously need to have this worked out in advance for several reasons: first, you're going to need to get the thing designed and printed, and secondly, it makes a handy blueprint for your wedding planner (or yourself) to structure and organize the rehearsal. As in all wedding documents, write a first draft early, and make revisions as things progress. Establish a deadline, working back from the printer to the designer, and give yourself some wiggle room. See to it that these are in the hands of the ushers prior to the wedding.

Recently I attended a wedding that also included a quick "what's next for the newlyweds" section of the program that laid out their honeymoon plans. Kind of cute, and probably useful so you don't have to answer that particular question ad infinitum.

The Wedding Party

There are traditionally certain duties attached to each of these roles. You may or may not want to respect tradition. Either way, it's good to make sure you let people know what's expected of them in the role – people don't always know. They may also expect to be following traditions, when you don't necessarily need or want them to. Like all good wedding traditions, you can ignore them. We've seen more and more weddings with "male bridesmaids" and multiple best men. It's all good. Don't let tradition force you into anything you're not excited about.

Make sure you ask people well in advance of the wedding, and give them time to make a decision.

Remember that it's traditional to buy each member of the wedding party a nice, small gift. It's easy to get caught up in this. Try not to get carried away, or overthink it. I got my groomsmen (and my father, the male ushers, ring bearer and officiant) small commemorative flasks, some booze, and some hangover remedies. Emma bought the bridesmaids lovely little pendants.

Maid of Honor

You wife is going to need to choose a maid of honor (or matron, if they are married). This role is, as it implies in the name, an honor. It is also a metric ton of work. The maid of honor is the *aide de camp* of the bride, handling a wide variety of roles both before, during and after the wedding. Traditionally, they organize the bridal shower (recording down the wedding gifts as they are opened). She helps organize the bachelorette party. She helps the bride buy her dress, shoes and accessories.

During the wedding, she traditionally handles the distribution of bouquets and boutonnieres. She keeps the groom's ring safe, she holds the bride's bouquet when needed. She manages the train on the bride's dress. She's expected to give a speech. She will process down the aisle with the best man. She also will act as an official witness to the marriage application.

There's not much you can do to help in the choosing of the maid of honor – it is your spouse's choice. Be supportive. If she asks for your opinion, offer it diplomatically. You'll want to develop a good working relationship with this person. Depending on how they responsible they are, you may need to cover some of their wedding planning tasks. At the very least you'll want to coordinate with your bride and the maid of honor that they have certain tasks covered, checking in with them often and offering lots of support. If they're in the same city, many of these tasks will be easier. If they are in another city, or you are having a destination wedding, it's not beyond the bounds of protocol to offer to help with various tasks. But take care: many maids of honor – believe it or not – relish these tasks and want to do them. Don't take them away from them without consulting them.

Though your influence is limited here, do what you can to encourage your better half to select a maid of honor that is energetic and responsible, and take care not to impose too stiff of a financial burden on someone who can ill afford it.

Bridesmaids

Being a bridesmaid seems to be a hell of a thing. A friend chooses you to assist them, to spend tons of money to be there for them, and in return you get to wear an ugly dress and not hang out with your spouse at a wedding. For months on end, you're supposed to abandon the traditional protools and morées of friendship and wait head and foot on an acquaintance who, up until now, was an equal. In theory, this temporary change in friendship dynamics is balanced out by an inverse, corresponding call to service in the opposite direction. That is, eventually this slave-driving bride will be your bridesmaid and you'll get paid back in kind. In reality, this rarely works out for a variety of reasons. People often have larger friend groups than the tradition accommodates, and rarely is the bridesmaid-duty exchange so directly one-to-one. Additionally, as you may have already noticed, people have an infinite variety of beliefs and habits relating to weddings, which in turn yield a wide array of possible expense outcomes for potential bridesmaids. In short, it's one thing to don your favorite little black dress, buy a bouquet and show up at city hall on a Tuesday afternoon (and, by the way, this is an incredibly fun thing to do in New York. I strongly recommend it). It's another to spend $5,000 to get to Fiji and another $2k on a Vera Wang dress you're never going to wear again. Is that a fair exchange? If you find yourself to be an easygoing type of bride, who wants a simple affair, the indignity of spending as much money on being a bridesmaid as you did on your own wedding can be profound.

In theory this is all balanced out, in some mystical nuptial equivalent of Karma – you're a bridesmaid a bunch and then you have a bunch of bridesmaids, and even if they're not the same people it's just all part of being a woman in modern America. We've only to look to the timeless adage "always a bridesmaid never a bride" to see even back in the day, the matrimonial Karma bank never quite balanced out.

But let's be fair. Being a bridesmaid can be a great experience. My friend Alex says she's been a bridesmaid often, and it was "not that bad." A ringing endorsement! She also says it can be "a great way to honor friends with a public way of showing how much you appreciate them." And this is very true. It is an honor. Our friends matter. I apologize for my cynicism. I simply mean to remind people to be sensitive to the obligations that we may be bestowing upon our friends.

The official duties of bridesmaids are relatively light: they assist the maid of honor in her tasks, chiefly the shower and the bachelorette party. They assist in little ways on an ad hoc basis. They process down the aisle with the groomsmen.

The Best Man

Your best man, traditionally, is responsible for the bachelor party planning and some body man duties the day of the wedding, most notably a great toast and the handing of the ring to the groom at just the right moment. Compared to the bridesmaids, the best man gets off insanely easy. Yet nonetheless, I still find it's easier, if you're a man planning your wedding, to just go ahead and take care of planning the bachelor party yourself. Take a moment here to think about how manifestly unfair it is that even though the man barely has any duties compared to the women bridesmaids, you're still going to save them from that duty. But hey, you're already doing your part for gender equality by planning the whole wedding, so don't be too hard on yourself. Your spouse, hopefully, will be similarly helpful with their bridesmaids.

There are a few duties you'll want to keep in the remit of your best man. He will process with the maid of honor, and hold on to the spouse's ring for you. He is to be an official witness to the marriage certificate, and to oversee the ushers on the day of the ceremony. Finally, you'll want your best man to handle the tipping of the staff. He will most likely be expected to make a speech at the reception. Assuming he's not a complete tool.

Even though they don't have much to do, it's a good idea to have a best man that is organized, kind, and communicative. As a wedding planner, you're going to have enough to do. If your best man can help with some of the stuff, all the better.

Groomsmen

When figuring out how many groomsmen you should have, you're going to need to work with your spouse here, but my advice is to simply match their number. If she wants 4 bridesmaids and a maid of honor, go with five-ish total yourself. You can be off by one it's not a big deal. If you have strong feelings on the matter and your future spouse doesn't care, you can be way off, with one of you having significantly more or fewer. Be prepared to handle some tricky logistics for the procession, but whatever, it's not rocket science.

Man Nup

Long ago in a galaxy far far away, the possibly apocryphal duties of the groomsmen were to ensure that the bride was not stolen away by bandits. This is, thankfully, less of an issue today, at least in America. Their present-day duties are relatively lighter: they often act as ushers, or assist the ushers. They process down the aisle with the bridesmaids. They tend to drink quite a lot. Furtively. From flasks. While wearing Chuck Taylors. It's a thing. And you know what? If those bandits do show up at your wedding these sneakered groomsmen will have your back.

The one piece of sartorial advice I can give here is that you don't need to make your groomsmen buy expensive clothes. Have them wear suits, and buy them matching ties. You're done. Maybe ask them to make the suits black. If you're asking for much more than that, beware of their financial condition. Every man should own a nice black suit. Beyond that, take care not to put too much financial strain on your best friends.

We have been seeing more and more weddings with bridesmaids and groomsmen of genders differing from the bride or groom, and I say more of this is welcome.

Families

Your parents and other honored or elderly

family members should also be felt included. This can often mean letting them walk the procession, including them in the program, and giving them corsage/boutonnieres.

This can be intense. Emotions run high around weddings. People have a lot of different emotions about weddings, and different people are going through different things in their lives. While some families are more drama-free than others, weddings in general are a time where families' emotions are fragile. Tensions may well flare. At its core, a wedding is an event where a bunch of people must gather at a certain time and place, regardless of everything else going on in their lives. It may be disruptive. It may be terrifying. It may depressing for them.

It's kind of amazing how many people pin their hopes and dreams in life on the fortunes and future of other people. Regardless of the advisability of such things, it remains true that many people may well have certain dreams and hopes pinned on your wedding. Parents will have pictures in their head of what their child's wedding was going to be like: cherished fantasies they've held since you or your spouse were born. These may be completely at odds with you and your other half's own plans.

As the wedding planner, you'll feel this especially keenly. You'll need to muster all of your diplomatic skills. Empathy and patience is important. Even as I write this, the urge is strong to get snarky and make digs about the improper things family members can do at weddings. Resist the urge as I am here. They're your family now, both yours and your future mate's. Do your best to appreciate their presence on your big day. Remember: whatever problems, neuroses and fear your family may have, they're overcoming these hurdles because they believe it's important to be there for you.

Your Spouse's Family

If you've got a bride, the bride's family traditionally pays for the wedding. These days, things are much more flexible. If your betrothed's family is paying for your wedding, they are going to have a say. If you and your future spouse are paying for the wedding, then you can decide, together, how much you're going to want to listen to them and coddle them. Regardless of the exact position of the line in the sand, that line needs to be drawn.

Remember, this is going to be your family. They are going to be in your life for a long time. They are not, however, yet your family, at least not the way your own family might be. There are things you can do to get your own family under control (and I use that phrase with some hesitation) that are not necessarily proper for you to do to your future spouse's family. Diplomacy will be important. It's also important to not come down too hard on your partner, imploring them to "get their family in line." Your partner is already aware of the challenges. Be supportive.

Mother of the Bride

The mother of the bride traditionally has a fair amount of responsibility. Her primary job is to help with the overall planning of the wedding, but that's really your job if you're reading this book. Still, even without this traditional role, there is much she can do. She plans the (or a) bridal shower. She helps with the selection of the wedding dress. If you have an engagement party, she traditionally hosts it.

Father of the Bride

Some families have a tradition of the father "giving away" the bride. Some choose not to do this – my wife declined to be given away – and, of course, some weddings don't have brides, so this may or may not be relevant to you. It could be bride and birde and two processions. No processions. Whatever you think is right. If the father is giving the bride away, he would process with the bride. Some brides choose someone else for the role of giving them away. This typically happens if their father is not present for the ceremony. This is pretty much in your future spouse's hands.

When the father of the bride is paying for the wedding, he gets to make a nice speech at the beginning of the reception, which kicks off the toasts of the reception. Many people choose to continue this tradition.

Your Family

Your father and mother traditionally would process in the ceremony. Their traditional roles beyond that are pretty light, relatively speaking. They might host a brunch the day after your wedding. They might make a speech or two. The previous words of caution regarding your future spouse's family apply here. Try not to get into fights with your family near your wedding day, and do everything you can to protect your better half from meddling parents.

The Rest of the Party

There are often a few other positions you might want to fill, depending on how many people you want to "feel involved."

Just last month I was at a wedding where there was a seven year old kid, especially assigned to high-five the groom as he walked into the room upon the presentation of the couple. It was magical. Consider the high-five kid.

The Officiant

The officiant is the most notable of these other participants in the wedding. In religious weddings, the wedding ceremony is performed by a priest, rabbi, pastor, what have you. In secular ceremonies, it's often someone that is close to both parties, perhaps having a hand in them meeting, or a good mutual friend. Someone with some gravitas. This has become a popular option in non-religious ceremonies, adding a nice personal touch.

Depending on the state you're in, this may not simply be an honorary position – they may have to actually perform a legal ceremony and sign the marriage license. You'll need to do your research on how far you need to go to make this happen. In some states, they need to be a legal pastor, which may mean getting a pastor's license from one of several online churches. Make sure the one your officiant chooses is recognized in the state you're performing the marriage in – not the one in which you reside. This can be a fair amount of time and paperwork, so make sure you choose your officiant in advance and give them easy-to-follow instructions on both becoming certified to be a pastor and to be an officiant. These are often two separate steps. If everything goes horribly awry, you can quietly get married at City Hall some period before the ceremony. Just don't tell anyone. You'll also want to work with your officiant in advance to prepare a full script for the wedding. After you say your personal vows, you'll probably want to have your officiant do one of the traditional vow exchanges and ring presentations. You can Google all this stuff and get it off the web and give it to your officiant, or let them wing it. Some people like to give the officiant a step-by-step guide of everything they should say, perhaps marking a spot for a few (brief) personal comments. Others like to let their officiant run wild. You and your betrothed should decide together.

The officiant either processes first or doesn't process. He or she runs the ceremony, speaking first and welcoming everyone. They ask the couple to say their vows (if they have prepared their own) and talks them through the formal vows. Gets to say "I now pronounce you..." or words to that effect. Processes out last or just smoothly disappears like a ninja when everyone's looking at the newlyweds.

Flower Boys and Girls and Ring Bearers

Traditionally, the flower person was a girl and the ring bearer was a boy. But times have changed and you can do what you want. Our flower person was an adult man and he did a stellar job. People laughed. Both can walk the procession, and both typically are right before the bride, or last-processing betrothed. You know, laying down beautiful flower pedals so angelic feet don't touch the dirty earth. That sort of thing. Feel free to include barnyard animals, but be considerate of guests' allergies. Nothing sours the mood faster than Aunt Rose's eyes swelling shut (again!) because of an ill-advised llama trotting.

Readings and Musicians

Many ceremonies have a reading (or two) or perhaps a musical performance. These are usually by close friends or family, not professionals. They may or may not process, but generally, they don't. They may be sitting up front or off to the side and they just show up when the time comes. Including a close personal reading can be very touching. It's also a great way to include someone who you care about who may not have another obvious role to play. If you're mic'ing your wedding, they are probably the one person who will need a second mic – you, your spouse and the officiant can share.

Ushers

Ushers are general assistants during the ceremony. They may seat the guests, hand out wedding programs, inform people of any last minute information, check coats and generally help out.

Traditionally, groomsmen play the part of ushers. But you can always have a few other people do it if you need to have a few people feel included. Beyond groomsmen, ushers can also be siblings, cousins, or friends. Get them corsages or boutonnieres and make sure you print their names in the program. One usher per fifty guests is a good rule of thumb. Not only that, as we discussed in the groomsmen section, you'll want enough boots on the ground in case of one of those bandit raids. So don't be stingy with usher assignments. Better them than you, if things get real.

Vows

Ten thousand years ago (okay, forty), a preacher man (or whatever type of religious official the religion at hand offered up) came up and told you to say some words, you repeated them, and then did the same to your partner. Once you were both done, they pronounced you married. Easy as pie. Simple, straight. I can't tell you the last time I was at a wedding where the sum total of the vows was the quick old litany and then boom, you're done. Interestingly, though, the litany is still there. I've noticed that of late, there's a sort of two-vow affair going on. We all grew up hearing the "with this ring..." schpiel, and we want it, but we also want to be special snowflakes who do things their own way.

I don't mean to be negative. I think it's quite nice. Here's the thing: the very meaning of marriage is changing. This is a how-to guide and not a philosophy book, but to put it simply, people get married for many different reasons and they want vows that reflect on the nature of their agreement. "To honor and obey" is not necessarily something most couples even want in the 21st century, though I'm sure my wife would be psyched if I vowed to obey, amirite? But seriously, folks. I crack myself up. But seriously. What does your marriage mean to you? Why are you doing this? What is important to say, right now, to your betrothed, and to the gathered love ones?

Take some time, write your own vows. It's traditional to keep these from your partner until the wedding day – we did. But, I mean, why, really? You can do what you want. It's a free country. For now, NSA, etc. etc. It's helpful to decide upon a word length, so one of you isn't talking for 10 seconds while the other talks for 40 minutes. That would be weird. But other than that, hopefully you both already have a good understanding of what it means for the two of you to get married, and your vows offer a chance to convey a personal, touching interpretation on that agreement. It's really one of the best things. You'll probably find yourself rewriting them all the day before you get married, that's okay. But write a first draft early.

Also, a word of advice. Don't include the traditional "speak now or forever hold your peace" line if you have even the teentsiest concern someone might take you up on it.

So What Happens

Ushers ush, music plays, people arrive, programs are handed out. Players gonna play play play. Haters gonna hate hate hate. You're going to miss all of this because you will be hidden away with your groomsmen (if they're not ushing), perhaps some family members, the day-of/week-of planner. You'll have worked out in advance the exact order of things from the rehearsal, and it will be documented in the program. Follow that. Breathe. Relax. Smile. Don't sweat it. You want to do this. It's all going to be fine. When you finally kiss your new mate, take a moment, smile at them, then look out and smile at everyone else. Breathe in. Enjoy it. Don't shake shake shake it off.

Chapter 12: The Reception

Time to Party

The ceremony has ended. You're married. Congratulations. Now let's party. We will start by walking through the various traditional components of a wedding reception, in the order of the timeline. Then we'll turn our attention to some of the more concrete logistical items: procuring the food and drink, venue selection, staffing and rentals.

Timeline

Your master timeline for the day should, it should be noted, also include the reception, as well as the time getting to the reception. You'll want to work out timing for things like when dinner is served, the cake cutting, the first toast, the last toast, the first dance: schedule every minute like it's an Apollo moon landing, or else your groomsmen will wander off into the street, down to the docks, and you'll never see them again.

Let's walk through the basic components of a wedding reception.

Cocktail Hour

Typically immediately after the ceremony (if you're using the same venue), or immediately upon guests arriving at the reception venue, there are some celebratory drinks. You'll probably miss these entirely. You'll be in some back room panting and kissing and thinking, "holy shit, I just got married." But as a good planner, you should make sure these are all properly organized in advance. Pick out some music. Perhaps a signature cocktail or two. Ensure that the ushers guide everyone into the proper location, if it's at the same venue. If it's at a different venue, be sure to include some directions in your wedding program. This is pretty run of the mill, so any wedding venue will know the drill. If you're having your Alaskan wedding in the wilderness or something, you'll need to arrange for this. Have the bar ready, and consider having some snacking food to tide people over till dinner.

You should allot 30 to 60 minutes for your cocktail hour: on the shorter side if they simply need to glide from ceremony room to cocktail room to dinner room. Also on the shorter side if they are arriving at a nearby, walkable venue, and the dinner preparation is ready to go in another room. Allow for additional time if there is room resetting that needs to be done (such as setting tables in the room you just used for the ceremony), or if travel time is substantial enough that people may be stuck in traffic. If switching venues, specify on the program exactly what time dinner will be served, especially if there is a gap. The more time you've given people between the ceremony and the reception, the longer people will respite before heading to the reception. They may try to sneak back to their hotel and sneak in a nap – especially if you're doing, say, an afternoon wedding and an evening reception. Let them know exactly when they need to be back.

Presenting the Couple

Somewhere during the cocktail hour, or immediately upon everyone being sitting for dinner, you should allocate a few minutes to "present the couple." Have your officiant, MC, or another member of the wedding party signal for everyone's attention. They will say something along the lines of "ladies and gentlemen, please allow me to present the new Mr and Ms. X." Or "Mr. and Mr. Y." There's a purpose to this, by-the-by. The format you use will let people know your new names: whether one of you has taken the other name, whether you've made up a new name, whether a woman is now Mrs. or Ms. Whatever change the two of you have contemplated post-wedding, this is the moment to announce it. Let the officiant know this as well. I've seen a few weddings where the officiant wasn't properly informed, and they just assumed the bride was changing her name, for example.

Then you pop in the room and wave like Jackie O. and John F., and everyone claps, and then you can hug people and generally feel marvelous. A coach of child-models once told me the trick to waving like a queen is to imagine you're spreading peanut butter. Hand flat, side-to-side waving motion with a bit of a curve to it. Very regal.

Reception Line and Making the Rounds

Do you want to do a reception line? The idea seems pretty nifty. Consider it. You can stand there and welcome each person as they arrive at the ceremony or at the beginning of the buffet line. Alternatively, you can make your rounds to each table during dinner, chitchatting with each guest along the way. That seems to be the en vogue thing to do in lieu of a reception line, but man, a reception line seems so much more classy. At any rate, unless your wedding is like 500 people, you should probably undertake one of these customs. It may be the one moment that you talk to some of the people at your wedding, and it's important to make them feel welcome. We didn't do this, owing to a 500+ person wedding, no assigned seats (yessss), and concerns about my wife being able to physically endure that much. But we missed it. I strongly recommend working this into both your physical logistics, as well as your timeline.

Dinner

Eventually your ushers (in their last official act) or the caterers will guide people to their seats for dinner. Consider some sort of formal notification, like the flashing of lights, an announcement from someone, or those adorable little wooden chimey-xylophones they use at the theater to let people know intermission is over. You can rent those things from your rental company, believe it or not. How's that for a touch of class?

It's good to apportion about 90 minutes for dinner in your wedding timeline.

Dinner is a substantially more complex affair than the cocktail reception. You have a few large decisions to make when planning the dinner. The first, obviously, is what to eat. We'll return to that topic anon. You'll also want to establish whether dinner is buffet style (cheaper, more casual), or formally served (generally more formal, more expensive).

Finally, you'll have to decide whether you are assigning seats and/or tables for your wedding dinner, or letting people sit where they like.

Man Nup

I will make no secret of my strong preference, as a wedding guest, to be allowed to sit where I like. I believe most wedding guests feel the same way. I will grudgingly acknowledge, however, that there are some practical benefits to assigning seats, such as knowing that you will have someone to talk to, and ensuring that your more introverted friends will be well tended to. The temptation to socially engineer your wedding through table, and even seat, placements can be extreme. If you do go this route, be judicious, and try not to micromanage or foist people on each other who may not get along but you really, really want them to. Another liability to assigning seats is that you are, in the end, to blame for any poor matches. People who aren't seated with people they like – or are seated with people with whom they don't get along – won't be able to help, just a little bit, blaming you for it. If your friends are particularly political, or you're involved in some sort of power structure in your society or town (perhaps you're Bruce Wayne), this can be particularly risky. People's egos can be ruffled by how near or far away they are sitting from you, and whether their rivals or peers have what maybe perceived as better seats. I know this can all seem insane and petty and, actually, it is. Which is why I forcefully advocate for chucking the whole practice in the garbage heap of history and letting people sit where they like. But if you choose to assign seats, you've been warned.

Consider this cautionary tale from Ryan, who endeavored to have assigned seats.

While my wife and I watched the pile of yes RSVPs tick past 200, we both got the sinking feeling that our seating arrangement had just crept up on the "things we were ignoring on the off chance they'd go away, but now are a serious f'ing issue" list. I'd recently lost the battle with my mother-in-law to host a "cocktail-style" reception, where our guests could mill around and sit themselves in the myriad nooks and industrial-chic crannies at the venue, and was now confronted with making an honest seating chart.

Two major issues surfaced for this exercise, 1) how to manage the list and the multiple revisions we were bound to undertake, and 2) how to actually shoehorn our various family and friend units into discrete groups to maximize the love and minimize the legendary passive aggression we'd incur from our Midwestern kin should we make a mistake and, God forbid, place our 2nd cousin fewer than two tables from their great aunt for.... Well, honestly I don't know, and you probably won't either.

Man Nup

I stopped resisting a fixed seating chart when I realized the following: I could use my benevolent power to seat family members at the same table who hadn't had the occasion to see each other in years and potentially – owing to health, time, life, etc. – may not have the chance sit together for dinner again. For our success in making that happen, I will be eternally grateful, and I imagine they will be, too. You, also, wield this power. Do so with pride and love.

You can also use this power to get your friends laid. Don't forget that. They won't. Which is actually the bigger point: your wedding reception will likely be the most opportune time to introduce your best friends to each other. They will get along, or they will at least pretend to get along on your behalf, and there's nothing more satisfying than being a friend matchmaker. It will pay you back. Remember, they all have something in common. They know you.

So hey. Maybe it's not all bad.

Certain types of people are tempted to go for assigned seats because the practice affords an opportunity for additional designed material – seat assignments and table cards – and even the chance to do something whimsical and fun with the seat cards. I've seen people use vintage records, little Japanese paper fans, chocolates and small stuffed animals as means of delivering the table number assignment to various guests. The whole thing can be quite adorable and quirky, gosh, and there's a bit of Pinterest-envy-level fashion going on with the practice. It also presents a fun method by which to deliver the gift that the new couple traditionally gives to each guest: oh, isn't it cute? Our table assignment is attached to this adorable wine stopper. To this, I say, bletch. Yes, it's all dandy, but I ask you, at what cost? Good god, man. If you want to do these fun things, set them out at the tables, or have some of your staff hand them out. You can enjoy the design benefits without putting people through the social awkwardness.

Regardless of which approach you take here, consider having a table assigned exclusively to family. They're old, they need a place to sit. Put it near you, at a place of honor.

Your Table

When arranging the whole tables at the reception situation, dedicate a table to yourself and your new spouse. This should be separate, but near, the family table. By yourselves. Just the two of you. You won't regret it. You're going to be pulled apart a lot during this reception. Having a table just the two of you to actually eat at, sit at, leave your stuff at, and not have anyone take your seat is really the nicest thing ever. It's like a one-night free bottle service for two, which is really quite a gratifying thing to get at your wedding. Have the servers serve you first, go to the head of the buffet line, or have servers discretely serve you from the buffet while others are waiting in line.

Toasts

Toasts are charming little speeches by your friends and family about how great you and your new spouse are, peppered with PG-13 anecdotes about times in your life you'd probably rather not remember. They're really quite touching and you might find yourself tearing up a bit, if you're a sensitive guy. That is, if you remember to give people warnings, so that they prepare. There are some roles that traditionally give a toast – the father of the bride, the best man, the maid of honor. And if you are NOT planning on having one of them speak, you might want to give them a polite heads up. For anyone who is speaking, though, it's good to remind them a few weeks before the wedding that they are expected to make a toast, and you are "looking forward to it." That should be enough to give them a polite reminder that you expect something of them. You can also go so far to say something like "we've got this baby scheduled down to the minute so do you think you can keep it under five minutes?" Most people of good common sense know this, but, hey. Since when did all our friends have common sense? Never hurts to remind them.

If you want someone else to speak for a toast – another family member, another groomsman or bridesmaid – you should ask them well in advance. "Would you do us the honor?" "It would mean so much to us." And give them the usual five minute polite hints. Don't spring it on 'em the day before the wedding. This therefore requires advance planning so make sure you have it covered: two weeks out from the big day, minimum.

Personally, I find the toasts to be most pleasantly delivered while we're all sitting around having dinner. Some people choose to do it later and stop the dancing-slash-reception and have the toasts then, but that's almost never as much fun. Toasts during dinner take a nice chunk of time I have to be making conversation with the other wedding guests you've stuck me at at this assigned table I dread so much. If you're going to do assigned tables, please, please, let's have the toasts while I'm awkwardly sitting there, so instead I can smile and nod and clap and mumble "hear hear."

Allot about ten to fifteen minutes per speech

in your wedding timetable. You might use less, but, hey. Some people like to ramble, bless their hearts.

Cake Cutting

The cake cutting is a ritual where the newlyweds get up there and cut the first piece of cake. Ancillary traditions include the relatively cloying one of each member of the couple feeding the other a piece of cake (tolerable but fine) and the tradition of stuffing the cake into each other's face. I'm tempted to say that the cake stuffing thing is horrible. Given the money spent, many brides would rather go blind than risk ruining their expensive makeup job, so in actuality any couple that figures out tolerable logistics of pulling this off ought to be applauded. I imagine it involves on-call makeup specialists and quick behind-a-curtain touchups, magic movie studio dissolving cake (does such a thing exist?), or skin like Scarlett Johansson. I've seen her in real life. Good god. Woman does not need makeup. But you know what? Even Scarlett Johansson probably has to wear makeup at her wedding, because even the most perfect skin can look a little ghostly in the over-contrasted black and white digital photography that seems all the rage at weddings at the moment. But I digress. If you can pull this off, props.

Man Nup

The cake cutting, by the nature of being a sort of "dessert kick off," necessarily has to proceed after dinner. This gives the wedding planner more leeway in when you actually schedule this in your timeline. You could do it right after dinner, much like a dessert in a restaurant, and that has some advantages: a captive audience, people being seated in predictable places so you can roll out a cake without risk of crashing into a drunken dancing guest. However, as flesh-and-bone food bags, humans are often quite full after dinner, so maybe it's good to wait. I find people are holding off on this tradition till a bit later in the evening more and more of late, taking a pause in the dancing to cut the cake. That, I think, is just ducky. Mark it in your timeline at a good place – say 30-45 minutes after dinner is ended – and have you or your planner coordinate with the DJ to stop the music and make an announcement. Allot 15 minutes for the cake cutting; most of that will be for awkwardly waiting for everyone to get back to the main area from the bar. Serve the cake from a serving station thereafter. Cake-cutting during dinner allows your serving staff, if you have them, to serve to individual tables rather than having a serving station free-for-all.

Man Nup

First Dance

The first dance and subsequent dances is a curious ritual. It is useful, as opposed to the infinite other number of things that they have yet to do for the first time together, because it allows you to then kick off the dancing/merriment portion of your wedding. It's a signifier to people to say "hold out a couple more minutes and all your polite obligations will be done and you can, from here on out, get drunk without worrying about additional duties," so people are generally looking forward to it. For that reason, it's probably worth doing despite the inherent ridiculousness of the act.

Some weddings include subsequent dances – usually father-daughter and mother-son. These are nice if you have a super close relationship with your parent, but are easily disposed of if your family is non-traditional, if people don't get along, aren't present, or you just don't want to do it for some other reason. I've seen them be quite touching when meant in a heartfelt manner, but they're often just sort of awkward. Choose whether it means a lot to you or your spouse and go for it, but only if you want to. It's totally acceptable to only do one of them and not the other. If, say, your spouse wants a dance with her father but you do not? Totally fine. The whole thing is really only worth doing if it will be touching. Otherwise people will be slowly edging towards the bar. These rituals can as well be applied to gay marriages – please, more father-son dances. Just what the world needs.

Dancing and Partying

This is what your groomsmen have been waiting for – when they can stop sneaking booze under the bleachers, and proudly drink in full view of the wedding community like the heroes they are.

Pretty much all obligations are done by this point (except tipping if you're handling that yourself), and from here on out you can chat and dance and drink and chill out. In your wedding schedule, this will be the balance of your time till the venue closes up shop.

Some people like to throw in a late night snack if the wedding is going long. Always a nice thing to do, but not absolutely 100% necessary, especially if you want to get this over with early. You can exhaust and inebriate your friends into comas, causing the party to peter out early. Or you can ply them with pizza or empanadas and keep things going all night. Your call.

If you haven't done a formal receiving line or an around-the-room during dinner, then do take time to make sure you talk to everyone, try to get everyone to dance, and generally make people feel welcome. Other than these moderate host duties though, you're entitled to enjoy yourself the rest of the night. Whew!

Afterparty

Many wedding venues close early – say, 10 or 11. If you want to party into the night, you may need to procure an afterparty venue. This is usually a nearby bar – or perhaps at the hotel bar of where your guests are staying.

This whole day will be very exhausting. Many people can't make it to their own wedding afterparty. That's okay. Take care to make sure that you don't explicitly PROMISE to anyone that you'll be at the afterparty. If you're feeling up for it, great. If not, don't sweat it. They will have plenty of fun without you. Having the afterparty at or near the hotel you are staying at makes it easy for you to pop upstairs to your room, get some alone time, rest, recharge and then hit the afterparty if you are feeling up for it.

The other great thing about the afterparty is you don't really have to pay for it. Book the room, hopefully with no fee. Or, failing that, just make a big reservation for a table at a bar or something, or pick a bar that is traditionally empty. Hotel bars close early. Coordinate in advance. Many hotels will accommodate a later bar for weddings that are using their facilities. Print the afterparty location on your wedding program. People expect to pay for their own drinks at the afterparty. Your obligations are done.

Man Nup

Chapter 13: In Closing

There you have it. Congratulations. Go forth, be fruitful and multiply. A few words of parting advice.

Don't forget to get into the photo booth. The odds are good these will be your favorite photos of you and your better half. There's something about the spontaneity, candidness and privacy that will make them intimate.

Pack a survival kit for your wedding. Everything you might need that night: cough drops, pain killer, throat spray (people find they are talking a lot), perhaps a flask. Put it all in a little man-purse and have your best man play body man, or stash it away somewhere safe (perhaps at your couple's table at the reception). Have whatever your bride might need on hand as well.

Don't get too drunk. The whole day and night will be long. You'll be pumped through with adrenaline, and you might think you can plow through. But not only do you not want to make a fool of yourself, embarrassing you and all your loved ones, you want to make sure you're present enough after it all for a few tender moments with your new spouse.

Don't do anything to encourage that glass clinking, kiss kiss thing. Ew. (pro-tip: it's hard to clink on plastic cups).

Don't worry if everyone else is having a good time. They will. Enjoy yourself, and work to make sure your partner is having a good time too.

Throughout this planning process, and especially on the big day, feelings are going to be a thing. This whole process is intense. On one level, it's just a big project planning assignment. But let's be honest with ourselves. It is more than that. It is love. It is our lives. It's the lives of the people that matter most to us. Emotions will run high. Try not to let them get the better of you.

But also try, on the big day, to be present. Many people look back on their weddings and wish they were more present. They wish they could remember it more. They wish it could have "lasted longer." Do as much planning as you can, in advance, and have other people handle as much as possible on the big day, so you can be fully present.

Remember to breathe. Remember to pause. To smile. To look out at everything and take it all in.

Remember to be attentive to your new spouse's needs. Remember to find moments for love and tenderness throughout the crazy day.

Man Nup

Don't speak too much, even if you planned and paid for the whole thing. No one wants to hear from you. And if they do, be classy and keep quiet anyway.

Remember to thank everyone that helped.

Remember to get your thank you cards out.

Put it on your calendar now.

Remember to tip everyone.

Send me a picture on Twitter.

Thank you, have a good night.

Man Nup

About the Author

Also by Rick Webb:
<u>Agency: Starting a Creative Firm in the Age of
Digital Marketing</u>.

Rick Webb is a writer and consultant to startups
and marketing companies. He grew up in Fairbanks,
Alaska, spent a goodly amount of time in Boston
and New York, and now lives in Chapel Hill, North
Carolina with his wife Emma and their cat Mrs. Fan-
nybottoms.

Follow Rick Webb on Twitter @rickwebb.

Or follow Man Nup, @mannupbook.

Sign up for Rick Webb's mailing list at rickwebb.net.

Read more of Rick's writing on Medium at https://
medium.com/@RickWebb.

Follow Rick on Facebook at https://www.facebook.
com/rickfordwebbington.

Acknowledgements

I'd like to thank Megan McCarthy, who told me one drunken night in the Lower East Side, "You should totally write a book about how you planned your wedding. For men." So here it is. Thank you, Megan, on behalf of all the men this book might hopefully help. I'd also like to thank my wedding planner, Jove Meyer, who not only contributed his time to an interview in this book, but saved my ass by coming in the week of my wedding and fixing every problem I wasn't yet even aware existed. Along with that, Jeremy Paredes, my friend and former coworker, who also has a secret career in wedding planning (who knew!) and contributed an interview as well. A thank you also goes to those wedding planning men who offered their insight and advice around wedding planning for men: Richard Blakeley, Mike Bodge and Ryan Navratil. Thanks to my advance readers: Morgan Holtzer, Don Huber, Ray Cha, Kristen Hawley and Christina Wallace. Thank you for my production partner, and publishing guru extraordinaire Gabe Stuart, who also helped out with the Kickstarter campaign. Thank you to Sean Drinkwater, who composed the hilarious music in the Kickstarter campaign. Thank you to Doug Pfeffer for some joke polishing – if you thought a particular joke was hilarious, it was probably his. If you thought it was terrible, it was probably mine. Thank you to the photographers: the first photograph in the front matter was taken by Storytellers & Co. The second one was taken by Eric Harvey Brown of Honey and Moon Photography. The back cover photograph was taken by Christopher Butler. All are used with generous Permission. Really. I am forever in their debt.

A giant freakin' thank you to our own wedding party: Sean Drinkwater, Jussi Gamache, Kristine Crosby, Abby Taylor, Clara Nguyen, Ashley Holtgraver, Kellianne Benson, Val Webb, Doug Pfeffer, Ryan McManus, Buster Benson, Aug Stone (thanks, too, to Aug for the title!), Andy Shea, Seth Hatfield, Brandon Hockle, Ben and Dan Bisceglia, and our wonderful parents Dick and Kathy Webb and Janet Wells.

Thank you to all of my friends who have invited me to their weddings in the past several years. I apologize for using your anecdotes and secretly taking notes at your weddings.

To my Kickstarter backers: Thank you thank you thank you so much. This would have been impossible without you. Abby Taylor, Adam Frank, Adam Miller, Aimee Hossler, Alex Tryon,

Alexandra Apostolou, Ali Berman, Alice Marwick, Alisa Richter, Alison Flood, Allison Mooney, Alyssa Newcomb, Amanda Kelso, Andrea Janko, Ann Weese, Annie Smidt, Anthony Dines, April Oelwein, Ari Levine, Ashley Jeanne Granata, Beau Smith, Benjamin Terris, Billy Linker, Blake Engel, Bonnie Greenwood, Brian Costello, Briana Campbell, Brooke Moreland, Bryan Gaffin, Buster Benson, Buzz Andersen, Cameron Walters, Carinna Tarvin, Chris Hinkle, Claire Armstrong, Cody Brown, Cole Rise, Cristina Hall, DLA Films, Dan Ingala, Daniel F Rowe, Daniel Schutzsmith, David Noel, David Ragins, David-Michel Davies, Deborah Singer, Diana Kimball, Doug Harmon, Doug Pfeffer, Elizabeth Stanton, Emily Taylor, Erica Kung, Erin Sparling, Eugene Leychenko, Eva McCloskey, G Scott Stukey, Gerard Ramos, Gibby Miller, Heather Morgan, Helena Price, Ian Westcott, Jamie Leach, Jane Rousseau, Jason Proctor, Jason Sack, Jay Sun, Jay Walsh, Jeff Lipton, Jennifer Sullivan, Jess Owens, Jessica Zollman, Jocelyn Malheiro, Jonathan Basker, Jonathan P Grubb, Jonathan Wegener, Josh Bis, Julian Missig, Justin Pierce, Justin Smith, Kathryn Yu, Kati Giblin, Keith B. Uram, Keith Butters, Kelly Reeves, Kenji Ross, Kevin Kwong, Kevin Lin, Kevin Talbot,

Man Nup

Kristen Hawley King, Kyle Rosin, Laura Gluhanich, Lee Dale, Leslie Chicoine and Lane Becker, Lexi Peters, Lindsay Wallner, Luke Marshall, Lynn Collette, Madeleine Di Gangi, Matt Raoul, Matthew Scott, Maya Baratz, Megan Peck, Melody McCloskey, Meredith Modzelewski, Michael Galpert, Michael Gatti, Michael Ma, Michael Williams, Michelle L. Dozois, Mick Lewis, Mike Paulo, Mike Bodge, Mike O'Toole, Mike Prevette, Mike Rubenstein, Molly Harding, Morgan Holzer, Nicholas Bonadies, Nicholas Hall, Nicholas Rhodes, Noah Brier, Orta Therox, Patty Mitchell, Rachel Henneck, Rachel Mercer, Ray Cha, Renee Zellweger, Richard Blakeley, Rob Allen, Ron Goldin, Ryan King, Ryan Lane, Ryan Mitchell, Sabina Batelman, Sam Valenti IV, Samantha Mastridge, Sarah Shimoff, Scott Beale, Scott Owens, Sebastian Bunney, Sharon McKellar, Song Hia, Stephanie Dub, Steven Lehrburger, Suzy Birmingham, Tara Strahl, T.C. Meggs, Terrence Curran, Tom Clifton, Tom Filepp, Tom Vongbandith, Vicki Adams, Vinnie Taranto, Will Hutson, William Weinand, and Yuri Ono.

Finally, thanks go to my wonderful wife Emma, who is responsible for this whole project when she said "if you want a large wedding that is just fine, but I don't want to plan it." On top of that, she also designed the cover. If you're interested in awesome graphic design – especially if you work on the X-Files, you can contact her here: https://twitter.com/emma-rocks.

Made in the USA
Middletown, DE
27 December 2019